Decisive Indian Battles and Wars

From Kurukshetra to Kargil

Savita Singh

ATLANTIC
PUBLISHERS & DISTRIBUTORS (P) LTD

ATLANTIC
PUBLISHERS & DISTRIBUTORS (P) LTD

7/22, Ansari Road, Darya Ganj, New Delhi
Tel.: +91-11-4077 5252, 2327 3880
E-mail: orders@atlanticbooks.com
Web: www.atlanticbooks.com

Reprint 2026

Published by Atlantic Publishers & Distributors (P) Ltd.

Printed & bound in India by Atlantic Print Services

Preface

Countless wars and battles have been fought on India's soil by various powers, but only a few of them can be called decisive, like that of the battle of Kurukshetra, fought between the Pandavas and the Kauravas—representing the world of the good and the evil, respectively—for establishing the true "dharma" instead of adharma, the evil. The history of India is replete with such examples.

The book includes 24 great wars, beginning with the battle of Kurukshetra (sometime between 5561 BCE and 800 BCE) and ending with the Kargil War, fought between India and Pakistan from May through July 1999. The battlefield of Kurukshetra, the vast plains, was chosen by the Almighty Himself, while the high-altitude mountainous terrain of Kargil was chosen by Pakistani soldiers, who in the garb of Kashmiri militants infiltrated across the India-Pakistan Line of Control.

The book is written to present India's history in an interesting way to the younger generations of today who have lost touch with it or know little about these decisive wars. The battles included in the book, among others, are the battle of Kalinga, fought by Ashoka the Great when he ascended the throne of Magadh, and in its aftermath of which he was so disillusioned that he became the disciple of Buddha and embraced non-violence for the rest of his life; the three battles of Panipat; the battle of Haldighati; the battles of Plassey and Buxar; the war of 1857; the Sino-Indian War of 1962; and the Indo-Pak Wars of 1965, and 1971, which led to the creation of Bangladesh. All these wars have been described very comprehensively.

The first battle of Panipat (1526) opened the doors of Delhi for the Mughals under the advancement of Babur. The second battle of Panipat (1556), fought between the forces of Akbar and Hemu—the Hindu ruler of Delhi—established a solid Mughal foundation in India. The third battle of Panipat (1761), fought between Ahmad Shah Abdali and the mighty Marathas under Peshwa Balaji Baji Rao, was the last battle between the two indigenous south Asian military powers until the creation of Pakistan in 1947. The main result of this battle was that the Maratha Empire never regained its stronger position in north India. This battle also gave the British an opportunity to step in against the weakened Marathas.

As recorded in history, the fierce battle of Haldighati, fought between Maharana Pratap of Mewar and the Mughal emperor Akbar on 21 June 1576, holds a unique place in the annals of Indian history. The Maharana was considered the Raja of all of Rajputana except Chittor. He refused to be crowned until he had won Chittor back from the Mughals, and declined to pay abeyance to Akbar or become his puppet. The other decisive wars described in the book also signify the establishment and beginning of an empire or the end of an era or empire as each one of them has been a turning point in India's history.

The exclusion of First and Second World Wars from the book is due to the fact that although India fought in them very valiantly and earned numerous decorations and gallantry awards, these wars were fought by it under the British rule and not as an independent nation. India salutes the cherished memories of those who laid down their lives in these wars by engraving their names inside the capital's India Gate.

To the reader of history, the battles of Wandiwash and Telicota will prove very interesting because of their far-reaching consequences. The battle of Wandiwash decided which foreign power was ultimately going to rule India—the French or the British—and the battle of Telicota rang the death knell of the powerful Vijaynagar Empire. Similarly, the battles of Plassey and Buxar, the Anglo-Sikh war, and the Mysore war described in the book will be an interesting reading for all.

Many historical events shown on television fail to give a true and comprehensive account of what had actually taken place and how it affected India. They also lack authentic sources. It is hoped that the book will set aside many of the myths and encourage younger generations and also the teachers, researchers and historians to delve deep into the history of India.

Savita Singh

Contents

1

CHAPTER

Battle of Kurukshetra

The famous Battle of Kurukshetra, fought between the forces of the five Pandavas and the 100 Kauravas, lasted for 18 days. Fought sometime between 5561 BC and 800 BC, it was considered the ultimate battle of the times—a battle between good and evil; right and wrong; *dharma* and *adharma*. In the original Rig Veda, there is a mention of the battle fought between ten kings. Some historians place the battle in 1339 BC or 3102 BC. According to Aryabhatta, the great mathematician and astronomer, the battle was fought in 3137 BC and was known as the Battle of Dharma. According to archaeological evidence, it took place sometime in 8th or 9th century BC.

Earlier on, known as Brahma-Varta, Brahmadevi or Dharamkshetra, how did Kurukshetra get its name? The story goes that eons ago, King Kuru came here on his golden chariot and this got magically transformed into a plough. Yoking this plough to Nandi, the bull of lord Shiva, and the buffalo of Lord Yama, King Kuru tilled the land. Lord Vishnu descended on the fields and asked Kuru to sow the virtues of mankind. Kuru shredded his right arm into a thousand pieces with Vishnu's *chakra* and planted the fields with the pieces. Vishnu granted Kuru two boons. One, the land would be named after him, and two, anyone dying there would go straight to heaven.

At present, in Haryana at Jyotsar, there is still a banyan tree that is supposed to be 5,000 years old and is supposed to have witnessed the celestial song of the Bhagwad Gita. About five kilometres from the present Kurukshetra on the Pehowa Road, in Narkatari village, there is a Bhishma Kund. Bathing in it is supposed to give one the combined merits of all the *tiraths*, or holy places.

The reasons that led up to the Battle of Kurukshetra were many. To understand them, it would not be out of place to give a brief summary of the epic Mahabharat itself. The writing of Mahabharat is credited to Sage Vyasa. It was recited by Muni Narad. The Kuru clan ruled the kingdom of Hastinapur. One of the earlier kings of Hastinapur, Shantanu, fell in love with and married goddess Ganga. She had imposed on him the vow that he would never question whatever she did. But when she had drowned seven of their new-born sons and was going to drown their eighth son, he could not help but stop her and ask why she was being so heartless. She immediately left both him and the baby and went away. This baby, Devavrat, grew up to become Bhishma. When Bhishma had been declared the heir apparent at the age of 16, Shantanu one day saw Satyawati, the daughter of Nishad Raj, the headsman of the fishing community. He fell in love with Satyawati, but Nishad Raj would not allow his daughter to marry Shantanu as he wished any sons from his daughter to become king after Shantanu. Devavrat, who was already heir designate, took a vow to give up all his claim to the throne of Hastinapur. But Nishad Raj was still not convinced that the children of Devavrat would honour his vow. So Devavrat took the vow of eternal celibacy and came to be known as Bhishma.

Shantanu had two sons from Satyawati, Chitrangad and Vichitravirya. After Shantanu's death, Chitrangad ruled for a short time and died of an illness. Then Vichitravirya was crowned.

The king of Kashi was holding the *swayamvar* of his three daughters: Amba, Ambika and Ambalika. A *swayamvar* is where a princess chooses her groom from the assembled rulers or men. Due to personal animosity, the king of Kashi did not invite anyone from Hastinapur. An angry Bhishma came and forcibly took away the three princesses. Ambalika and Ambika agreed to marry Vichitravirya, but Amba declared that she was already in love with Salvyaraj, the king of Salvya. So Bhishma sent her to him with all honour, but Salvyaraj refused to marry Amba and sent her back to Bhishma, saying that she was no longer free. An angry Amba then went back to Bhishma, asking him to marry her as, according to her, he was responsible for her plight, but Bhishma gave his vow as an excuse and refused to do so. Amba cursed him and vowing to take her revenge in the next birth, went into a jungle and committed suicide by immolating herself.

Vichitravirya also died without an issue. Satyawati asked Bhishma to procreate with the two queens of Vichitravirya so that Hastinapur could get an heir. Bhishma refused, citing his vow of celibacy. A desperate Satyawati asked her illegitimate son from Rishi Parashar, who had turned into a sage, Vyas, to help the two queens of Vichitravirya to get sons. Vyas agreed. But he had been meditating in the forest for some time and looked so fierce that Ambika shut her eyes when with Vyas and, so the story goes, her son, Dhritrashtra, was born blind. Ambalika turned pale while with Vyas; so her son, Pandu, was born yellow, or jaundiced and weak. Seeing this, Satyawati asked Vyas to try once more. Both Ambika and Ambalika refused to go and sent their maid instead. So was born Vidur, healthy, wise, intelligent and a major character in the Mahabharat. He went on to become the prime minister, or *mahamantri*, to both Dhritrashtra and Pandu.

At the time of the carnation of Dhritrashtra, who was the eldest Kuru son, Vidur stepped in and stopped the ceremony, saying that no blind man could become a ruler. So Pandu was crowned. Pandu married Kunti and Madri, while Dhritrashtra married Gandhari, who tied a bandage upon her eyes for the rest of her life so that she could share the sightless world of her husband. Gandhari's brother, Shakuni, was angry that Bhishma and others had forced his beloved sister to marry a blind man. He vowed to destroy Hastinapur. So he came and took up residence in Hastinapur.

One day, while out for hunting, Pandu by mistake killed a sage and was cursed that if he consorted with a woman, he would die. So far, he had no issues. Kunti, in her young days, had pleased the sage Durvasa and had got a boon from him. She could call on any god once and get a son from him. Eager to test the power of the boon, she had already tried it once on the Sun God and had had Karna. To avoid being labelled an unwed mother, Kunti had put Karna in a wicker basket and set the basket afloat on a river. The child had been found by a poor, childless charioteer Adhirath, and his wife Radha, and was brought up by them. Now, Kunti got three sons. From Dharma, the god of justice, she got Yudhisthir. From Vayu, the god of wind, she got Bhim, and from Indra, the god of heaven, she got Arjun. She shared her boon with Pandu's younger wife, Madri, who got Nakul and Sahdev from the Ashwini Kumars. Pandu died when he could not help himself and broke his celibacy with Madri. Feeling responsible for his death, Madri committed sati, leaving Kunti to bring up the five Pandu brothers, who came to be known as the Pandavas. Kunti returned to Hastinapur, where the Pandavas were brought up with their cousins, who were known as the Kauravas. These were the 100 sons of Dhritrashtra. The eldest was known as Suyodhan but later came to be called Duryodhan because of his black deeds, and his younger brother was known as Dushasan. The other Kaurava brothers who were also well known were Sukarna and Vikarna.

Pandu's son Yudhisthir was older than Duryodhan, the eldest son of Dhritrashtra. Dhritrashtra was ruling in the name of Pandu as his representative when Pandu had gone for relaxation to the jungles and also after he had passed away and the children were all too small.

Right from childhood, there was a lot of rivalry between the Kauravas and Pandavas. Duryodhan could not stand the Pandavas and even tried to murder Bhim, but Bhim got saved. Once the children were old enough, it was decided that to avoid conflict, the kingdom of Hastinapur would be divided. Dhritrashtra gave Varnavrat to the Pandavas. Here, Duryodhan got a palace made out of lacquer and planned to burn it down along with the Pandavas. But they were saved by sage advice from Vidur. They went into hiding. While they were hiding, the marriage of Draupadi took place in an unusual way with all the five brothers. The Pandavas returned to Hastinapur and established their kingdom at Khandvaprashtha, and called it Indraprastha.

Duryodhan, seething with rage because the Pandavas had escaped the fire, invited the Pandavas for a game of dice. He won the entire kingdom from Yudhisthir in a rigged game of dice. He then took his revenge on the Pandavas' common wife, Draupadi, who had once insulted him by calling him blind like his father, by asking Dushasan to strip her in public—Lord Krishna saved Draupadi from humiliation by ensuring that she could not be stripped. When an angry Draupadi started to curse the Kauravas, Gandhari pleaded to her for mercy for her sons and stopped her from cursing her sons and forced Dhritrashtra to give back everything to Yudhisthir. But once again, Duryodhan won everything from Yudhisthir in another game of dice and now sent the Pandavas into exile for 13 years followed by one year of living incognito. After they had completed this exile, with many an adventure, and demanded their kingdom back, Duryodhan refused to give it back. When they said that they would be satisfied if he gave them only five villages, he refused to do even this and declared that he would not give them any land, not even one as small as the tip of a needle, leave alone five villages. Thus, war was declared from both sides. The armies of the Kauravas and Pandavas met in the planes of Kurukshetra and fought for 18 days.

The location of the ancient Kurukshetra lies in modern-day Haryana. Some of the kings who took part in the battle were Prgjyolisha (Assam), Avanti, Dakshinaapatha, Yavanas, Sakas, Matra, Kaikeyas (border of Afghanistan and Pakistan), Sindhus, Sauviras, Panchalas, Kosala, Kasi, Magadha, Matsya and Yadus. The two armies fought every day from dawn to dusk. In those days, they had what was called the *chaturang sena*, consisting of *paiks* (or foot soldiers), *raths* (or chariots), *asvas* (or cavalry), and *hastis* (or elephants). The core of the *chaturang sena* was the chariot, made of wood and leather, drawn by horses and carrying an archer. The first three components had been there earlier, and elephants were introduced in about 1100 BC. The advantage the elephants had was that they could be used in rocky and swampy areas.

The Kauravas had 11 divisions, and the Pandavas had seven. A division was called an akshauhini, and each akshauhini consisted of 21,870 chariots; 21,870 elephants; 65,610 horses; and 109,350 foot soldiers. All in all, 3.94 million men fought from both sides. The weapons used were bows and arrows, maces, spears, daggers and swords. Arjun, Bhishma, Drona, Karna, Kripacharya and Abhimanyu favoured the bow and arrow. Duryodhan and Bhim favoured the mace. Yudhisthir's favourite weapon was the spear.

In Mahabharat, most of the battle is described by Sanjay, the charioteer of Dhritrashtra, who had been granted *divya dhristi*, or extrasensory powers, for the duration of the battle to see the battle from where he sat and describe it, giving a blow by blow account of it to the blind Dhritrashtra.

On the first day of the battle, Duryodhan appointed his great-grand uncle Bhishmapitamah as commander-in-chief of his army while the Pandavas appointed Draupadi's brother, Dhristadyumna, as the commander-in-chief of their army.

Just before the battle started, Arjun of the Pandavas became sentimental, refusing to fight. He refused to lift arms to kill those who were his relatives and many of whom he loved and respected and in fact revered. Lord Krishna, who was his charioteer, then gave his famous discourse from the Bhagavad Gita. He exhorted Arjun not to let his sentiments get in the way of his duty but to fight for truth, honesty, virtue and goodness. He told Arjun in no uncertain terms that if evil stands in the way of good, or *adharma* is pitted against *dharma*, it is the duty of a warrior to fight evil and *adharma*, disregarding all ties and relationships, however close they are to him.

Even in those days, there were rules of war like the Geneva Convention today. Both sides had to adhere to them. Some of the rules laid down were that fighting would only last from sunrise to sunset. After that, everyone was free to visit each other or tend to the wounded. People could only fight with someone equal to them and holding a similar weapon. There would be no fighting with a woman or a child. A fighter who was unconscious or down would not be attacked. A warrior who had surrendered had to be treated honourably as a prisoner of war and not killed or harmed. Death or capture of a leader signified defeat. Night attacks on sleeping warriors were forbidden. So was mean, deceitful and cruel behaviour forbidden.

But war has always been a dirty game. Even in those days, it was no better. Although called the battle for *dharma*, Mahabharat saw the use of foul means, deception and sneak attacks. Knowing fully well that Karna was invincible with his *kavach* (shield) and *kundal* (power rings worn in the ear) and also that he was her firstborn, whom she had abandoned, Kunti took advantage of his well-known generosity to take these away from him so that her younger son Arjun would not be at a disadvantage.

On the 12th day of war, Arjun was lured away by Shrisharma, the king of Trigartadesa. The Kauravas tried to capture Yudhisthir while Arjun was away but failed to do so. So, on the 13th day of the war, Arjun was lured away once more and Dronacharya set the *chakravyuh*. As no one could penetrate it except Arjun, who had been again lured away, Arjun's son Abhimanyu offered to do so. The story goes that while Abhimanyu's mother, Subhadra, had been expecting him, his father, Arjun, had once described to her how to get into a *chakravyuh* but Subhadra fell asleep before he could tell her how to get out of it (recent studies have proven that this is not too farfetched a theory. A child learns a foreign language faster if the mother had been subjected to hearing the language while the child was still inside the womb and that children do react to their mothers' voices reading out to them while still in the womb). So Abhimanyu only knew how to get in but not how to get out of a *chakravyuh*. While inside the *chakravyuh*, when he lost his chariot and was without arms, he was surrounded by the Kauravas and killed in the most unmerciful way against all the conventions of war. Jayadrath, the brother-in-law of the Kauravas, was the first to strike a blow on the unarmed boy. When Arjun returned and found out what had happened, he vowed to kill Jayadratha by sunset the next day or immolate himself. When on the next day they found that Jayadratha had been hidden away, given full protection by the Kauravas, Lord Krishna, the master of deception, used his powers to create an eclipse-like situation, giving the illusion that the sun had set and the battle was over for the day, so that Jayadratha would emerge from hiding. That is what happened. Thinking himself safe, Jayadratha emerged and jeeringly asked Arjun to get ready to fulfil his vow of immolating himself. At that moment, Krishna lifted the illusion and the sun emerged. Krishna urged Arjun to kill Jayadratha as the sun had not yet set. At the end of the war, Dronacharya's son, Ashvathama, to take revenge for the death of his friend Duryodhan, sneaked into the Pandavas' camp and killed Draupadi's five sons, thinking they were the Pandavas. Again, when Bhishma began to prove invincible to the Pandavas as he had the boon of death by desire, the wily Krishna suggested that they put a woman in the field as Bhishma would not fight a female. In lieu of a woman, which would have been against all the conventions of warfare, the Pandavas put Shikhandi, who was a eunuch and whom Bhishma considered a reincarnation of princess Amba, on Arjun's chariot. On seeing Shikhandi, Bhishma immediately laid down his arms.

On the 10th day, when Bhishma Pitamah fell and was laid out on the bed of arrows, Guru Dronacharya took over the command of the Kauravas' army. He was equally powerful. The Pandavas again removed him by deception. Bhim declared that he had killed Ashvathama—actually an elephant but also the name of the only beloved son of Dronacharya. When Dronacharya asked for confirmation from Yudhisthir, who was supposed to be truth and piety incarnate, Yudhisthir is supposed to have said, "Ashvathama *hatha* (elephant) *kunjara* (is dead)." But when he said the word "*hatha*", Lord Krishna blew his conch shell, drowning out his voice. The result was that a heartbroken Dronacharya thought he had indeed lost his son and wanted to immolate himself. But even before he could do this, Draupadi's brother, Dhristadyumna, chopped off his head.

Karna, who was actually the eldest Pandava, although himself a very honourable and noble soul, fought on the side of evil to repay his debt to Duryodhan, who had been the only one who had supported him when he was being insulted in the arena where the princes had been demonstrating their skills. Duryodhan had made him the king of Ang Desh. When Karna's chariot sank in the mud and he had to get down to pull it out, on the urging of Lord Krishna, who reminded Arjun that Karna was one of the men who had killed the weaponless Abhimanyu, Arjun killed him in cold blood, though it was against the tenets of war.

Duryodhan fought till the end. When in the final stages he was pitted against Bhim, Lord Krishna once again helped and indicated to Bhim to hit below the belt, in the area Duryodhan was vulnerable. So both sides played tricks, and all the Kauravas but one (Vikarna, who had switched to the side of the Pandavas at the beginning of the war) died and the Pandavas won. It was considered a victory for *dharma* as represented by the Pandavas. But it was a costly victory. Draupadi lost all of her five sons. Bhim lost his son Ghatothkach, from Hidimbaa. Arjun lost his son, Abhimanyu, from Subhadra. Many great warriors like Bhishma, Dronacharya, Kripacharya and Duryodhan died. War is a situation in which both sides lose. The vanquished lose, and so do the victors. Everyone is impoverished and made poorer only.

References

1. Chopra, B.R. (Producer), and Chopra, B.R. and Chopra, R. (Director). (1988). *Mahabharat* [Television series]. Mumbai: B.R. Films.
2. Khosla, M. (2002). *Kurukshetra: Mahabharata Country*. Retrieved from http://www.the-south-asian.com/aug2002/Kurukshetra.htm
3. Roy, K. (2004). *India's Historic Battles: From Alexander the Great to Kargil*. Delhi: Permanent Black.
4. Wikipedia (n.d.). *C. Rajagopalachari*. Retrieved from http://en.wikipedia.org/wiki/C._Rajagopalachari
5. Wikipedia (n.d.). *Kurukshetra*. Retrieved from http://www.dharmakshetra.com/holy%20land/kurukshetra.html
6. Wikipedia (n.d.). *Kurukshetra war*. Retrieved from http://en.wikipedia.org/wiki/Kurukshetra_War

2 CHAPTER

Battle of Hydaspes

The Battle of Hydaspes, as the Macedonians of Greece called it, was fought on the banks of Jhelum (the Greeks called it Hydaspes), in India, between Alexander the Great of Macedonia, in Greece, and Porus, the king of the Hindu kingdom of Paurav. It was fought on the banks of the Jhelum, a tributary of the Indus in Punjab, near a place called Behra, which is now in Pakistan. It was the most costly battle fought by the Macedonian satrap, but it opened up India to Greek political and cultural influence for centuries to come, which is evident from the Greco-Buddhist art, which has come down to us through the centuries.

Alexander III of Macedonia, one of the greatest military leaders of history, on par with Caesar, Genghis Khan, Timur and Napolean, was born on 20/21 July 356 BC in Peela. He was the son of Philip II. As a young man, he was tutored by Aristotle till the age of 16. He created one of the largest empires of the ancient world, which stretched from the Ionian Sea to the Himalayas.

Alexander succeeded his father, Philip II, when the latter was assassinated in 336 BC. Alexander was given the generalship of Greece. Two years later, in 334 BC, he invaded Persia. He ruled Asia Minor and started off on his carrier of campaigns, which lasted ten years. He defeated the Persian king Darius III and conquered the Persian Empire. After this, his own empire stretched right from the Adriatic Sea to the Indus River.

Alexander's role model was his father, Philip, whom he saw always winning and going on in spite of getting injured.

Alexander always wanted to outdo his father. There is evidence that he many a time deprecated the achievements of his father to his friends, showing a bit of jealousy on his part. Alexander also had a great thirst for knowledge and loved philosophy. He was an avid reader, very intelligent and a quick learner. He had great charisma, and the very force of his personality made him a great leader. Unfortunately, he also loved his drink a lot.

Alexander was an unparalleled general. He always made the best use of the available terrain, phalanx and cavalry tactics. He was bold and enjoyed the fierce loyalty of his men. He was a shrewd commander and used the *sarissa*, a spear that was 20 feet long. This had been perfected by Philip II. Alexander liked it for its reach, speed and manoeuvrability.

Alexander had an amalgamation of forces under him. To unify them, he himself joined them in every battle. He was also a master of adapting his tactics and techniques to outdo the style of his opponents. In India, to counteract the force of war elephants, which the Greek forces had never seen, he allowed them to come forward by opening his ranks. Once they had advanced, he surrounded them and his soldiers used the *sarissa* to strike upwards and dislodge and kill or wound the mahouts, or the elephant controllers.

King Porus, the king of Paurava, which lay between the rivers Jhelum and Chenab, now in Pakistan, was probably the descendant of the Puru tribe. He was a handsome man, all of 7 feet tall and very brave also. He himself led the last and final charge in the battle.

After the defeat of the Persian Achaemenid Empire's forces under Bessus and Spitmenes in 328 BC, Alexander began a new campaign to extend his empire towards India. In May 326 BC, he approached the Hydaspes River, which was in spate due to the rains at that time and impossible to cross. He camped on the west bank of the river.

King Porus, learning about Alexander's intended attack, martialled his army and gathered on the east bank of the river. Unable to cross the river at that point, Alexander looked around for a favourable place from where crossing would be easier.

He found this near Jalalpur, about 17 miles away, where there was a small footbridge strong enough to allow the infantry, cavalry and supply trains to cross over. The Macedonians used skin floats filled with hay and rafts to make a silent crossing in the dead of the night when a storm was raging. To deceive the enemy, Alexander left a small contingent at his base camp with a minor official dressed like him wearing the king's cloak moving around so that the enemy would think the Macedonians had not moved out.

A small detachment of Alexander's cavalry attacked and pillaged the towns and villages near Jalalpur. Porus's got the impression that it was a small Macedonian contingent and sent a small detachment of 3,000 men and 100 charioteers under his son Raja to investigate. Believing it was a small detachment, Raja, turned his entire army towards them. But as they ploughed deeper, Raja realised that Alexander, in a pincer movement, had surrounded them. Raja lost his life trying to get out. Only 200 of his men made it back.

Porus now pulled back 10 miles to a level place, where war elephants and cavalry would have place to manoeuvre. Here, Porus, in the traditional battle style, arranged his infantry on a wide front supported by chariots and cavalry. He positioned himself in front of the main infantry line, just left of the centre, with the war elephants on his right.

Alexander had his cavalry on his right wing and his infantry phalanxes to the left of the cavalry. Alexander had also concealed 1,000 of his cavalry to the right of his flanks, behind some bushes round a bend. They had orders to only attack when the Indian right wing was totally involved with Alexander's exposed left flank, which was being used as bait.

Alexander's army consisted of 13,000 infantry and 3,000 cavalry. Porus's army consisted of 31,000 infantry, 4,000 cavalry, 200 chariots and an equal number of war elephants.

Alexander opened the battle with his mounted archers attacking the Indian left flank. Porus launched his left-wing chariots and cavalry. The chariots proved no match for the swiftly moving Macedonian horsemen, who swept them aside.

The cavalries collided, and a fierce battle ensued. Porus launched his war elephants against Alexander's extreme left flank. The Macedonians had never seen elephants before. The Greeks advanced in a lock-shield formation in a solid wall. They fought out of sheer fright and either killed the mahouts or hamstrung the animals, i.e. injuring them in the legs with their pikes, wounding the animals, which spooked the animals into backing out and trampling their own soldiers. But the Macedonians were also totally mauled. Porus saw his chance and ordered the right-wing chariots and infantry to attack. At this point, Alexander signalled his hidden cavalry to come out and attack. They came out from behind the charging Indians and attacked. These fresh units turned the tide. Alexander's general, Parmenio, ordered the left infantry phalanxes forward. Porus was trapped. There was a major attack going on from the front, his left wing was falling back and, on the right, his forces were being cut to pieces. At this point, Porus could have retreated but decided to lead from the front. As they collided, the Macedonians had an advantage with their 20-foot-long pikes. Porus fell. Instead of surrendering, the Indians fought harder to save their leader. In the centre, only troops were left. The left wing crumbled and melted away. The right flank was swept aside and destroyed. Porus still fought beside his troops, but his officers, fearing for his life, abducted him and took him away forcefully. His troops fought with renewed vigour to help him escape. Alexander was surprised at this fanatical devotion to a king and the refusal to surrender. In this battle, the Indians were left with 20,000 dead and 5,000 were taken prisoner. The Macedonians lost 3,000 men. According to historian Arrian, the Macedonians lost only 310 men. Diodorus puts this figure at 1,000 men. According to him, the Indians lost 12,000 and 9,000 were captured. Eighty war elephants were also captured.

According to the historian Justin, there is a story that during the battle, Porus challenged Alexander directly—who charged upon the back of his horse. Alexander fell, and his bodyguards carried him away and captured the injured Porus.

The next day, Alexander sent a message to Porus and asked for a meeting. When Porus came, Alexander is supposed to have asked Porus how he would like to be treated. Porus replied, "Treat me, O Alexander, like a king."

Alexander did just this. He treated Porus well and allowed him to keep his kingdom and rule it in Alexander's name. Porus lost no wealth, rank or part of his kingdom. He was allowed to keep them all, including a small standing army to defend himself against his enemies. In return, he and Alexander vowed to help each other in times of need.

In this battle, Porus made mistakes after mistakes and that is why, in spite of having a much bigger force than Alexander had, he lost the battle. Firstly, he never took the initiative but kept waiting for help from his ally Abhisar, the king of Kashmir and Himachal Pradesh.

Porus never anticipated that the attack would be launched on a dark and rainy night, when it was least expected. His intelligence was woefully poor. Alexander had the advantage of operational surprise. Porus had no idea that the main army of Alexander had landed and not just a scouting party, which was a big intelligence failure.

Porus misjudged the strength of the enemy that had crossed the river. He held back most of his troops and sent a small contingent under his son to tackle them.

Porus was undoubtedly a brave man, and so were all his generals and men. But there was no cohesiveness between them. They all functioned as individuals and not as a unit.

As Porus's army consisted of various contingents from various states and they were not a cohesive, professional, standing army, for them to operate and do collective manoeuvres was very difficult. Each contingent was under its own ruler. There was no proper chain of command. If the leader died, there was no one to take over.

The Greek army was better equipped as its cavalry used armour like breastplates and steel helmets, while the cavalry of Porus had only cloth *pugrees*. Although the saddle had yet not been invented, the Greeks used blankets on their horses, which gave them a better grip and better control, while the Indians rode bareback.

The Greeks were better equipped. Their spears were nearly double in size to those of the Indians. The Greeks were better tacticians also. Their phalanx attack was such that the army of Porus found itself herded together in a tight group, unable to manoeuvre.

The lessons from this battle later led Kautilya, the greatest military theoretician in Indian history, to emphasise training and planning before a battle.

This was the last major battle fought by Alexander. After this, he founded the city of Nicea on the spot where the battle was fought on the east bank of the river Jhelum and another city, Alexandra Bucephalus, to honour his brave horse, who died soon after this battle. Alexander had ridden this horse in every battle of his in Greece and Asia.

In 326 BC, Alexander approached the boundaries of the Nanda Empire at Hyphasis (modern-day river Beas, at Kathgarh in Indora tehsil of present-day Himachal Pradesh). From here, he turned back as his weary troops rebelled. They did not want to go forward anymore. So Alexander turned back to return to Macedonia but died of food poisoning on his way back. They say that the town of Alexandria was built on the place where he died.

References

1. Roy, K. (2004). *India's Historic Battles: From Alexander the Great to Kargil*. Delhi: Permanent Black.
2. Wikipedia (n.d.). *Alexander the Great*. Retrieved from http://en.wikipedia.org/wiki/Alexander-the-great
3. Wikipedia (n.d.). *Indian Campaign of Alexander the Great*. Retrieved from http://en.wikipedia.org/wiki/Indian_campaign_of_Alexander_the_Great
4. Wikipedia (n.d.). *King Porus*. Retrieved from http://en.wikipedia.org/wiki/King_Porus
5. Wikipedia (n.d.). *Battle of the Hydaspes*. Retrieved from http://en.wikipedia.org/wiki/Battle_of_the_Hydaspes

3

CHAPTER

Battle of Kalinga

The Battle of Kalinga was fought between the Mauryan Empire, under Ashoka the Great, and the state of Kalinga—a feudal republic situated on the present-day coast of Odisha and partially in northern Andhra Pradesh. Kalinga City, the capital of the kingdom of Kalinga, is situated at present-day Srikakulam, in Andhra Pradesh. In earlier times, the kingdom of Kalinga stretched from the Damodar, a tributary of the Ganges, in the north to the Godavery in the south, and from the Bay of Bengal in the east to the Amarkantak range in the west. There is mention of Kalinga in the Mahabharat also. The then king of Kalinga, Srutyan, fought on the side of the Kauravas. Megasthenes, the Greek historian, has mentioned Kalinga in his book *Indica*. According to him, both Magadh and Kalinga in those days were Jain-dominant kingdoms. He also states, "The royal city of the Calingae is called Parthalis. Over their king 60,000 foot soldiers, 1,000 horsemen, 700 elephants keep watch and ward in precinct of war."

Originally, during the Nanda rule, Kalinga come under Magadh suzerainty. But when the Mauryans came to power, Kalinga broke away and became independent. This was considered a real setback and loss of political prestige for Magadh. In keeping with the traditions of the time, Ashoka's grandfather Chandragupta Maurya had expanded his kingdom from Assam and Bengal in the east to Afghanistan and Baluchistan in the west. His empire included Nepal and Kashmir in the north and extended to the Deccan in the south. He was the first emperor to unify India to such an extent. But when he had attempted to recapture Kalinga, he failed to do so. Chandragupta Maurya was the only king to have held out against the army of Alexander the Great. Later on, he abdicated and become a Digambar Jain monk.

Ashoka was the grandson of the great Chandragupta Maurya, the founder of the Mauryan Empire. He was the son of Bindusar and Dharma, a commoner, who was the daughter of a Brahmin belonging to the Ajivika sect from the city of Champa. Ashoka was born in 304 BCE and came to power in 273 BC. It is said that he killed 99 of his brothers to secure the throne for himself. But he was crowned only in 269 BC, four years after coming to power.

As a young man, Ashoka was brave, bold, troublesome and cruel. He loved hunting and was known to have killed lions with just a stick. His brothers connived against him and got him posted to Taxila, where he gave a good account of himself by putting down a rebellion. Ashoka was once again exiled to Kalinga for two years, where he fell in love with a fisherwoman, Kaurwaki, whom he married.

After this, Ashoka was sent to Ujjain, where he got injured while quelling an uprising. His brothers had plotted once again to get him killed; so he went into hiding. He was tended to secretly by Buddhist monks. It was here that he got introduced to Buddhism and learnt its basic tenets. Here, he met another girl, Devi, who was involved in looking after him while he lay injured, and he married her too.

When Bindusar was dying, he wanted another son of his, Sushim, from another wife, to succeed him. But Ashoka had the backing of the ministers because Sushim had been arrogant and disrespectful towards the ministers. Ashoka got rid of his rival by tricking him into entering a pit full of live coals.

In his early years, Ashoka was bad tempered and wicked to boot. He made his ministers prove their loyalty to him and when they failed, he got 500 of them killed. On another occasion, he is said to have burnt alive 500 of the women in his harem when he felt they had been disrespectful to him. He also built an elaborate building that came to be known as Ashoka's Hell. This building was beautiful on the outside, but the tortures carried out by his executioner Girikaa inside were worse than hell. Thus, he got the name of "Canda Ashoka" or "Chandaa Ashoka", meaning "Ashoka the fierce" or "Ashoka the terrible".

Professor Charles Drekmeier warns us to take all references to the fierceness and evilness of Ashoka prior to his conversion with a pinch of salt. Maybe the Buddhists exaggerated it a little to show up the change in his personality by his dramatic conversion to Buddhism, brought about after the Battle of Kalinga.

Although Kalinga had given shelter to him when he was in exile and one of his wives was from there, Ashoka had no compunction in attacking it in his desire for revenge and expansion.

The Battle of Kalinga was the only major war fought by Ashoka after he ascended the throne of Magadh. It was one of the bloodiest battles in the history of India. In its aftermath, Ashoka was so affected by it, so moved by all the carnage, that he became a Buddhist who opposed violence and embraced *ahimsa* for life.

The causes which led up to the Battle of Kalinga are varied. Although the Magadh Empire stretched from the Hindu Kush in Afghanistan to Bangladesh and Assam in the east and to Kerala and Andhra Pradesh in the south, it had no good ports. It was dependent upon its neighbours for access to the sea, and all trade had to be routed through the ports of Kalinga. The Kalingans gave brutal treatment to traders coming from Magadh. Again, in those days, expansionism was the norm. Every king who came to power tried his level best to expand the boundaries of his kingdom. Ashoka was no exception. He wanted the Kalingans to accept his suzerainty. They were too proud to do so. They had held out against Chandragupta and Bindusar and thought they could hold out against Ashoka also. At that time, Ashoka was himself a brutal and arrogant man. The man who had killed 99 of his brothers for the crown was definitely not going to allow the arrogance of the Kalingans to go unpunished. He wanted revenge.

Eight years after he ascended to the throne, in 261 BC, Ashoka declared war on Kalinga. The two armies met on the banks of the river Daya. It is claimed that it was such a bloody battle that the river, which runs alongside the battlefield, turned red with the blood of the slain. According to the history, around 150,000 warriors of Kalinga were slain and Ashoka lost 100,000 of his own men.

Dhaula Hill in Bhubaneswar, Odisha, next to the Daya River is considered the location of the battle. Here, there is a major edict, edict number 13 of Ashoka, engraved on a mass of rocks that lie by the side of the road that leads up to the summit of the hill. This edict states:

> "Beloved-of-the-Gods, King Priyadarshi, conquered the Kalingas eight years after his coronation. One hundred and fifty thousand were deported, one hundred thousand were killed and many more died (from other causes). After the Kalinga had been conquered, Beloved-of-the-Gods came to feel a strong inclination towards the Dharmma, a love for the Dharmma and for instructions in Dharmma. Now Beloved-of-the-Gods feels deep remorse for having conquered the Kalingas."

Priyadarshi was another name for Ashoka.

Ashoka should have been happy and edified by his victory in the Battle of Kalinga. He had crushed the Kalingans completely. But, surprisingly, all the death and carnage had the opposite effect upon him.

The story goes that the morning after the battle, a woman approached Ashoka and said, "Your actions have taken from me my father, husband and son. Now what will I have left to live for?" Ashoka was moved by these words so much and filled with so much guilt and remorse that his victory turned sour in his mouth.

Another version goes that the day after the battle, Ashoka was walking through the city of Kalinga and saw only bodies, burnt houses, crows, vultures, and destruction. He was horrified and disgusted with the death and carnage he saw all around him. He started wondering if victory was worth all the horrifying destruction and carnage. He is supposed to have reproached himself by intoning:

> "What have I done? Is this victory, what's defeat then? Is this victory or a defeat? Is this justice or injustice? Is it gallantry or a rout? Is it valour to kill innocent children and women? Do I do it to widen the empire and for prosperity or to destroy the other's kingdom and splendour? One has lost her husband, someone else a father, someone a child, someone an unborn infant...what's this debris of corpses? Are these marks of victory or defeat? Are these vultures, crows, eagles the messengers of death or evil?"

The brutality of the conquest sickened Ashoka and turned him. He lost all desire for expansionism. This, in turn, led him to embrace Buddhism, whose tenets he had imbibed when the Buddhist monks had looked after him while he lay injured in Ujjain. They had saved his life when his brothers would have had him killed if they had found out. He remembered the selfless devotion of the monks, their sacrifice and their gentle outlook and respect for all life forms. Sickened by the number of deaths, he felt his desire for revenge and expansionism was responsible for them. He give up violence all together and eschewed *ahimsa*, and although he annexed Kalinga and kept it in his kingdom, he never again killed or encouraged killing in any form. He banned live sacrifice and hunting for sport. He became a vegetarian and banned the burning of forests and agricultural waste, which may harbour wild animals. He banned tortures like gouging out of eyes and the death penalty as punishment. He pardoned the elderly and those who bore the responsibility of families. He advocated respect for others, even servants. Although an advocate of Buddhism, he fostered respect for all religions and his subjects were free to follow any religion they chose to.

According to *Ashokavadana*, a 2nd century CE text that relates to the legends of Ashoka, he sent *bhikshus*, or monks, as Buddhist envoys to various countries far and near. He sent Madhyamik Sthavira to the modern Kashmir and Afghanistan. Maharakshit Sthavira was sent to Syria, Persia/Iran, Egypt, Greece, Italy and Turkey. Massin Sthavira was sent to Nepal,

Bhutan, China and Mongolia. Sohn Uttar Sthavira was sent to modern Combodia, Laos, Myanmar (which in those days was known as Swarnbhumi), Thailand and Vietnam. Mahadhhamarakhhita Sthavira was sent to Maharatthha, or the present Maharashtra. Maharakhhit Athavira and Yavandhammarakhhita Sthavira were sent to south India. He sent his two children from Devi, a son called Mahindra and a daughter named Sanghamitra, to modern-day Sri Lanka.

He ruled peacefully for the next 40 years. He died at the age of 72. He established many vihars, like Nalanda and Taxila. He constructed the Sanchi and Mahabodhi Temples. In *The Edicts of Ashoka: An English Rendering*, by Ven. S. Dhammika, it is stated:

> "Now it is conquest by Dhamma that Beloved-of-the-Gods considers to be the best conquest. And if (conquest by Dhamma) has been won here on the border, even six hundred yojans away, where the Greek King Antiochus rules, beyond there, where the four kings named Ptolemy, Antigonos, Magas and Alexander rule, likewise in the south among the Cholas, the Pandyas, and as far as Tamrapani. Here in the king's domain among the Greek, the Kambojar, the Nabhakas, the Nabhapamkits, the Bhojas, the Pitinikas, the Andhras and the Palidas, everywhere people are following Beloved-of-the-Gods instructions in Dhamma. Even where Beloved-of-the-Gods envoys have not been, these people too have heard of the practice of Dhamma and the ordinances and instructions of Dhamma given by Beloved-of-the-Gods are following it and will continue to do so."

In modern times, we in India have adopted many of the symbols of Ashoka. The Ashoka Chakra in the middle of our flag is a depiction of the Dhamma Chakra, the Wheel of Dharma of Ashoka to be found upon the famous Ashokan pillars. It has 24 spokes. Of these, 12 represent the 12 laws of dependent origination, and the other 12 represent the 12 laws of dependent termination. Ashoka made many pillars, out of which only 10 survive. Each of these pillars was 40-50 feet high and weighed approximately 50 tonnes.

Originally, the pillar at Sarnath had the Lion Capital of Ashoka on top, with a Dhamma Chakra above it. The Lion Capital consists of four Indian lions standing back to back, and they were adopted in 1950 as the emblem of India. Each of the pillars has been carved out of a single piece of polished sandstone quarried at Chunar, which lies just south of Varanasi. There is his famous Iron Pillar at Kutubminar, which has not rusted since then.

References

1. Dhammika, V. S. (1993). *The Edicts of Ashoka: An English Rendering.* The Wheel Publication No. 386/387.
2. Szczepanski, K. (n.d.). *Ashoka the Great.* Retrieved from http://asianhistory.about.com/od/india/a/ashoka.htm
3. Wikipedia (n.d.). *Ashoka.* Retrieved from http://en.wikipedia.org/wiki/Ashoka#Early-life
4. Wikipedia (n.d.). *Lion Capital of Asoka.* Retrieved from http://en.wikipedia.org/wiki/Lion_Capital_of_Ashoka
5. Wikipedia (n.d.). *Kalinga (India).* Retrieved from http://en.wikipedia.org/wiki/Kalinga (India)
6. Wikipedia (n.d.). *Kalinga War.* Retrieved from http://en.wikipedia.org/wiki/Kalinga_War

4 CHAPTER Battles of Tarain/ Taraori

The Battles of Tarain, or Taraori, were fought in AD 1191 and 1192 near the town of Tarain, or Taraori, near Thaneshwer in present-day Haryana, which is about 150 kilometres north from Delhi. They were fought between the Ghurid forces, led by Sultan Shahab-ud-din Ghori, and the Indian forces, led by Prithviraj Chauhan.

Sultan Shahab-ud-din Muhammad Ghori, originally known as Mu'izzuddin Muhammad Bin Sam, was born in AD 1150 to Baha-ud-din Sam Bin Hussain, the local ruler of Ghor. He was a ruler of the Ghurid dynasty, which ruled Ghor for 500 years. He laid the foundation of Muslim rule in India. He ruled over present-day Afghanistan, Pakistan and India.

Muhammad Ghori was the younger son and began his career as a general under his brother Ghiasuddin Ghori. A strategic warrior, he had deep interest in art and culture. He recaptured the city of Ghazni from the Oghuz Turks in AD 1173 and thus brought to an end The Ghaznavid Empire and started the Ghorid Empire. He remained the governor, and his brother Ghiasuddin remained the Sultan until he died. Muhammad Ghori became very unpopular as he had to impose heavy taxes. As his sources started drying up, he started looking around for other sources and he started looking at India as at that time India was the richest country in the subcontinent.

Ghori consolidated his empire fast. In AD 1175-76, he captured Multan. Three years later, he invaded India and turned south towards Gujarat. Here, in the Battle of Kayadara, he was soundly defeated and withdrew. Three years later, he went back and in AD 1181 took Peshawer and Sialkot. Then, he allied himself with the ruler of Jammu, Raja Vijaya Dev, and in AD 1187 took Lahore.

Prithviraj Chauhan III, generally known as Prithviraj Chauhan, was from an agnivesh Rajput clan—one of those clans that were born from the sacrificial, or yagna, fire. He was the last independent Hindu ruler of Delhi before Hemu. He came to the throne in AD 1169, at the tender age of just 20. He ruled from both Ajmer and Delhi. He had got the throne of Delhi from his *nana*, or maternal grandfather, Arkpal, or Anangpal III, of the Tomar dynasty of Delhi, and Ajmer was the capital of his father's Rajput kingdom of Chittor. He controlled much of present-day Haryana and Rajasthan. There is a controversy about who his mother was. According to one version, Anangpal Tomar II of Delhi had two daughters, Roopsundari and Kamladevi. Roopsundari was married to the king of Kannauj Vijaypal and had a son Jaichand. Kamladevi was married to Someshwer Chauhan, king of Ajmer. She had a son Prithviraj and a daughter Pritha. According to some sources, Prithviraj's mother was Karpuri Devi, a Kalachuri (Chedi) princess and the daughter of Achlaraja of Tripuri, and Jaichand was the grandson of Govindchandra Gahadwala (Rathod) of Kannauj. This bit of information becomes of value later on because Prithviraj eloped with Samyukta, the daughter of Jaichand. But that is another story.

In AD 1181, Ghori seized Sialkot. In AD 1186, he seized Lahore, and in AD 1191, after seizing Peshawer, Mohamad Ghori laid siege to Bhatinda, which was on the outskirts of Prithviraj's kingdom. Prithviraj appealed to his father-in-law Jaichand, but Jaichand was still smarting from the way Prithviraj had made a fool of him on the occasion of his daughter's marriage. Jaichand was the ruler of Kannauj. Prithviraj and Jaichand had become sworn enemies. The story goes as follows:

In AD 1175 Jaichand decided to hold a swayamvar for his daughter Samyukta, also called Sanjogita. Samyukta had heard tales of Prithviraj's bravery and valour. Impressed by them, she decided she would marry him and no one else. A swayamvar meant that all the eligible kings were invited and Samyukta could choose whom to garland and marry. Jaichand, out of sheer spite, did not invite Prithviraj, and to add insult to injury, he put a statue of Prithviraj at the door to represent a *durban*, or guard. Samyukta sent a message to Prithviraj, who came in disguise and stood near the statue. Samyukta walked down the line of waiting and expectant kings and garlanded the statue of Prithviraj, who immediately came out of hiding and pulling her up behind him on his horse raced away. Jaichand gave chase but was unable to catch the pair. He never forgave the pair for making a fool out of him, and so he refused to help Prithviraj and, in fact, helped Muhammad Ghori. Undaunted, Prithviraj sent a huge force under his vassal Govind Raja of Delhi, who marched to Bhatinda, and the battle took place at Tarain, near Thanesar and it came to be known as the First Battle of Tarain. At that time, Prithviraj was holding Ghori's brother as hostage. Ghori obviously wanted to rescue his brother and get Prithviraj to set him free.

Ghori tried to use the tactics Mahmood of Ghazni had used before in history. He divided his forces into three flanks and personally led the central flank on horseback. Prithviraj Chauhan had double the number of foot soldiers and about 300 war elephants. Ghori's men had never seen elephants. Ghori led two regiments in an attack on the centre. He met Govind Raja in personal combat. Govind Raja lost his front teeth to a lance thrown by Ghori. But his forces were exhausted and ran out of water and were routed. Prithviraj's forces chased Ghori and his men for 40 miles. Ghori was injured and was captured and brought in chains to the capital of Prithviraj. There, on his pleading, Prithviraj released him respectfully and Ghori returned to Lahore and then to Gajni to lick his wounds. This was the biggest mistake Prithviraj made.

The Second Battle of Tarain

Ghori consolidated his empire. He appointed his *mamulak*, or slave, Qutb-ud-din Aibak commander and returned to challenge Prithviraj in AD 1192. Prithviraj was complacent after his victory of AD 1191. Prithviraj had 50,000 infantry and 20,000 cavalry. The Muslim army consisted of 35,000 cavalry, which included some camels, 20,000 infantry and about 1,000 rear guards.

According to the Persian historian Farishta, the Indians had 3,000 elephants and 300,000 cavalry and infantry.

But this time, Ghori had come prepared. He attacked the rear lines of Prithviraj, completely out-flanking him. Prithviraj's cavalry counter-attacked, forcing Ghori to retreat, but Prithviraj did not follow up on his advantage. Ghori's light cavalry attacked Prithviraj's flanks. This halted Prithviraj's men, and there was confusion in his army. His troops got boxed in, and, thus, even though his forces were numerically superior, there superiority was neutralised.

The allies of Prithviraj let him down. Ghori sent a message that his brother should be released and that Prithviraj should accept defeat and convert to Islam. Prithviraj refused. But then, without waiting, and against all the then existing tenets of war, Ghori attacked Prithviraj before sunrise. In those days, it was the unwritten law that fighting would only take place from sunrise to sunset. The Rajputs followed this unwritten rule, which in all probability came down right from the time of Mahabharat and Ramayan.

Ghori divided his forces into five parts. He attacked early in the morning, while the Indian soldiers were still not ready. Ghori sent waves after waves of mounted archers. The Indians hastily got ready and advanced. As Prithviraj's war elephants advanced, these archers retreated. Sultan Ghori deployed four parts of his army to box in Prithviraj's army, and the fifth was kept in reserve. General Khande Rao, alias Govind Raja, of Prithviraj's force was killed. At dusk, Sultan Ghori himself led a force of 12,000 heavily armed cavalry to the centre of the Rajput lines, which collapsed. Prithviraj was taken prisoner.

Within a year, Ghori was controlling north Rajasthan and the Doab region between the Ganges and the Yamuna, and the Raja of Ajmer became his vassal. In Lahore, he made Ali Karmakh governor. Till then, Ali Karmakh had been governor of Multan. Here, in a glittering durbar, he conferred the title of Aibak, meaning "axis of faith", on Qutb-ud-din. Qutb-ud-din Aibak took Ajmer in AD 1193. Soon, Rajput kingdoms like Saraswati, Samana, Kohram and Hansi were all subjugated. He captured Delhi after the Battle of Chandwar, where he defeated his previous ally Jaichand by a surprise attack. Ghori's armies, under Turkish generals, raided as far east as Bengal. Aibak ransacked temples in Ayodhya in AD 1193. Ghori left Qutb-ud-din Aibak as his naib-us-sultanate in India before he returned to Ghazni to deal with unrest on his western frontier.

According to *Prithviraj Raso*, unlike Prithviraj, who had treated Ghori with respect, Ghori did not treat Prithviraj well and took him to Ghor as a prisoner. He brought Prithviraj to court and when Prithviraj looked him proudly in the eye, Ghori asked him to lower his eyes. Prithviraj replied arrogantly that a Rajput only lowered his eyes in death. Ghori was incensed and got him blinded by red-hot pokers. After that, every day Prithviraj was brought into his court, where the other courtiers made fun of him and mocked him. At this time, Prithviraj was joined by his court poet and biographer Chandbardai, who had written Prithviraj's biography in poetry form known as *Prithviraj Raso*. Both men were upset by Ghori's treatment of Prithviraj, who was considered one of the best warriors in India and probably in the world in those days. They decided to take revenge if they could. They got the opportunity when one day, Ghazni decided to hold a competition in archery. Prithviraj asked permission to take part. Ghazni and his courtiers laughed at him but on Prithviraj's insistence allowed him to do so, thinking it would provide another form of sport. On the day of the competition, he asked Prithviraj how he would shoot when he could not see.

Prithviraj asked him to give the command. Ghori was suspicious. "Why do you want to only shoot on my command?" he asked.

"Because a Rajput king only obeys the orders of another king," replied Prithviraj. Satisfied, Ghori was giving the command when Chandbardai intoned four lines of a poem, "*Char bans, Chaubees gaj, angul ashta praman, ta uppar Sultan hai, mat chuko Chauhan.*" (The length of four bamboos, twenty-four yards and eight fingers width, the sultan is sitting. Do not miss him Chauhan.)

Prithviraj shot Ghori in the head and killed him. Instantly, Ghori's bodyguards caught Prithviraj and killed him too.

But other historians give a more prosaic version of Ghori's death. They say Ghori was assassinated on March 15, 1206 while he was offering prayers at Damik near Sohawa, near the present-day city of Jhelum in Pakistani Punjab, by either local Gakharis or Hindu Khokars.

This was the beginning of the Muslim rule in India. For the next six centuries, Delhi remained under Muslim rule, until in 1858, when the last Mughal ruler Bahadur Shah Zafar was exiled to Rangoon. The Battle of Tarain laid the foundation of the Sultanate of Delhi. But the Muslim rule for a long time, and for the most part, was confined to Delhi and its surroundings in UP. The Tomars of Gwalior and the Ranas in Mewar continued to rule in central India. Man Singh Tomar of Gwalior stoutly resisted the Lodi's and stopped the southward march of Sikander Lodi at Gwalior. The kingdom of Chittor, the centre of Prithviraj Chauhan, and which was the centre of most of this resistance, held out even during the Mughal rule.

Why did Prithviraj lose in spite of having a much larger force at his disposal? There was no lack of bravery or personal courage either where the Hindu fighters were concerned. Prithviraj lost mainly because the Hindus have always been divided by factions. They become weak because of infighting and mutual conflict. They were never cohesive. Their military methods were out of date. The Muslim cavalry was quicker than the lumbering war elephants. The Muslims were better organised and had better leaders. They, in fact, had two types of cavalry. The first was used for skirmishes and was the light cavalry, and the second, with heavier armour, was used as shock troops for charging. The first fought with light bows and arrows from far. The second wore coats of chainmail as body armour, which were less cumbersome than the solid body armour used by the Indians, and had steel helmets known as *khods*. The

Hindus were always defensive and complacent. These were the very factors that caused the Chinese debacle in 1962.

Again, Prithviraj was leading a confederacy with no central authority. So the Rajputs, in effect, were headless as Prithviraj himself was equal to the other leaders in his confederacy and not considered the supreme leader. Once the battle started, Prithviraj could not control all the factions under him. He had in fact a divided command, which is always dangerous.

Again, the Turks were already used to fighting elephants, so the advantage of these cumbersome fighting animals was lost to the Indians.

In short, it is not the size of the force that is crucial in deciding the outcome of a war but the techniques and the nature of technology that determine the outcome. The Afghans used naptha fire to spook the elephants and eliminate the advantage they gave to the Indians. When faced with this, the frightened elephants trampled their own soldiers in their desire to get away.

References

1. Hinduhistory (2008). *Prithviraj Chauhan.* Retrieved from http://hinduhistory.blogspot.in/search?q=prithviraj-chauhan
2. India-Forum (n.d.). *The Second Battle of Tarain.* Retrieved from http://www.india-forums.com/forum_posts.asp?TID=744541
3. Indianetzone (n.d.). *Muhammad Ghori, Medieval History of India.* Retrieved from http://www.indianetzone.com/4/muhammad_ghori.htm
4. Roy, K. (2004). *India's Historic Battles: From Alexander the Great to Kargil.* Delhi: Permanent Black.
5. Wikipedia (n.d.). *Battles of Tarain.* Retrieved from http://en.wikipedia.org/wiki/Battle_of_Tarain
6. Wikipedia (n.d.). *Mu'izz al-Din.* Retrieved from http://en.wikipedia.org/wiki/Muhammad_of_Ghor
7. Wikipedia (n.d.). *Prithviraj Chauhan.* Retrieved from http://en.wikipedia.org/wiki/Prithviraj_Chauhan

5

CHAPTER

The First Battle of Panipat

The First Battle of Panipat was fought between the forces of Zahir-ud-din Muhammad Babur Timrud—a descendant of Timur from his father's side and a descendant of Genghis Khan, also known as Changez Khan, from his mother's side, and the ruler of Kabulistan—and the forces of Ibrahim Lodi, ruler of the Lodi Empire in Delhi. Fought on April 21, 1526, at Panipat in today's Haryana, it was one of the first battles in which gunpowder, firearms and artillery were used.

Babur was born on February 14, 1483, in the town of Andijan in Fergana Valley, which is in contemporary Uzbekistan. He was the eldest son of Omar Shekh Mirza, the ruler of Fergana, who was the grandson of Timur. Babur's mother was a descendant of Changtai Khan, the second son of Genghis Khan. Babur came to power in the province of Fergana in the year 1494 at the tender age of 12. He had a very active life and won many battles before he came to India.

Ibrahim Lodi was the youngest son of Sikandar Lodi and was the sultan of Delhi in 1526, at the time of the First Battle of Panipat. The Lodi dynasty, which was also known as the Ludi dynasty, consisted of both Afghans and Pashtuns. It ruled India from 1451 to 1526. It was founded by Bahlul Khan Lodi in 1451.

Ibrahim Lodi was a fearless military leader. He was capable, laborious, just and caring as a ruler. He really desired the welfare of his subjects. There are many stories about his personal courage. There is the story in which his own uncle Alam Khan and the governor of Punjab, Daulat Khan Lodi, attacked Delhi in 1525. They destroyed the main army of Ibrahim Lodi, but Ibrahim Lodi refused to leave the battlefield. Next morning, he observed the men of his enemies looting and pillaging. He attacked them and not only stopped them but also sent them packing.

Unlike his father, Ibrahim Lodi was also rash, not very savvy politically and failed to understand the psyche of his nobles and senior ministers. He was adamant and failed to compromise and make peace with his nobles, thus alienating them. He sacked all those whom he suspected of corruption or betrayal and appointed younger men who were loyal to him. This action threatened the very self-respect of the nobles who had been in power so far. This provoked them to rebellion and led to direct conflict between the nobles and Ibrahim Lodi.

Ibrahim Lodi was also surrounded on all sides by enemies: the Khilji dynasty to the northeast, the Rajputs to the northwest and the Sultanate of Gujarat blocking all access to the sea on the east. Khandesh and Berar blocked the south. These included Jaunpur, which lies in present-day Uttar Pradesh.

Sikandar Lodi wanted his elder son, Jalaluddin, to succeed him upon his death. But the nobles supported Ibrahim Lodi. His brother rebelled, but Ibrahim Lodi, with the help of the governor of Bihar, Dariya Khan, defeated him near Jaunpur.

Babur considered the lands belonging to the Lodi dynasty as his as he was the rightful heir to Timur's throne. Timur, when he had attacked India, had won Delhi and other estates and had left Khizi Khan, his vassal, in charge of Punjab. Khizi Khan had later declared himself sultan of Delhi and founded the Sayyad dynasty but had himself been ousted by Ibrahim Lodi, a Ghilzai Afghan. Babur sent in many expeditions to India. Once he came as far as the Indus but then went back as the Indus was in spate and it was impossible to cross it in enough strength to attack Hindustan and Delhi. Babur had already taken control of Punjab before his last expedition into India.

Babur's fifth, and final, expedition to Hindustan began late in 1525. His control on Punjab was being threatened by his former ally Alam Khan, who was the uncle of Ibrahim Lodi. Alam Khan had returned to Lahore from Kabul earlier that year and joined up with Babur's enemy Daulat Khan, the former governor of Lahore during the reign of Ibrahim Lodi and who, for a brief time, had been Babur's ally. At the time Babur left Kabul, Alam Khan and Daulat Khan attacked Delhi. The forces of Ibrahim Lodi defeated them. Daulat Khan surrendered to Babur, while Alam Khan joined him in his march to Delhi.

With Punjab secured, Babur advanced towards Sirhind, and thence to Ambala. He sent a detachment, under his son Humayun, to fight a detachment of Ibrahim Lodi at Hisar-Firuza. Humayun defeated this detachment on February 26, 1556.

From Ambala, Babur moved east, to Jamuna at Ambala itself. He then turned south and defeated another of Ibrahim Lodi's armies in the Battle of Doab on April 2, 1556.

Babur Timurud defeated the much bigger forces of Ibrahim Lodi, the sultan of Delhi. Babur's forces numbered 15,000 men and 20-24 pieces of artillery. Babur had acquired muskets and artillery guns from the Turks, including gunpowder and the technology of how to make the best use of it. In those days, the muskets and the big guns were not very accurate. Nor were they very safe. They failed if the gunpowder became wet, or many a time, the barrels burst, killing those firing them. The barrels of the big guns had to be stuffed with gunpowder contained in a sack. Then, the big boulders used as projectiles were stuffed in. A sharp instrument made a hole in the powder bag from a hole on top of the barrel. A bit of gunpowder was sprinkled around the hole. When orders to fire were given, a lighted fuse was put down the hole. Once the fire reached the sack of gunpowder, this was ignited and, with a big boom, shot the projectile out. Some of the guns could fire as far as a mile but were not all that accurate, although they were devastating.

Ibrahim Lodi had about 100,000 men. Although the fighting force consisted of only about 30,000-40,000 men, the rest were camp followers. He also had 1,000 war elephants. Babur's forces had never fought against war elephants. But Babur remembered stories from his boyhood about Timur and Alexander and how they had turned the war elephants of their opponents by targeting the elephants and their mahuts (handlers) and frightening the beasts so that they turned on their own soldiers.

Babur's field artillery proved decisive in the First Battle of Panipat. Ibrahim Lodi had none, and the sound of the cannons frightened the war elephants. The elephants, who had never faced such a thing, became out of control and turning, ran amok and trampled their own men. Babur's tactics carried the day. He used the tactics of *tulughma* and *araba*. *Tulughma* meant dividing the entire army into various units, that is, the left, the right and the centre. The left and the right divisions were further divided into the front and the rear divisions. Each of these worked as an independent unit and could be used to surround the enemy. *Araba*, meaning carts, were provided to the forward centre division. Babur gathered 700 of these. These carts were placed in a row facing the enemy and, in the Ottoman style, were tied to each other, but instead of chains they were tied with ropes made out of animal hide. Between each pair of carts, six wooden tripods were set up. The matchlock men supported their matchlocks upon these to fire. There was enough space left between each cart for archers hiding behind them to fire arrows and for two or three mantlets to be erected, behind which were located the guns. Mantlets were huge, shield-like structures on moveable wheels. These mantlets were such that when required, they could be used to move the cannons and easily manoeuvre them. Again, enough space was left at intervals for 100 to 200 riders to ride through. The combination of these two tactics made Babur's army lethal. The guns and cannons could be fired and yet protected against enemy fire by the *arabas*, which were held in place by the ropes connecting the carts. The aim of the nozzles of the guns could also be changed fast with the help of the mantlets, which were on wheels.

Babur's formation was protected on one side by the town of Panipat and on the other side by bushes and ditches. He also used Timur's battle plan of digging trenches and using the mud taken out to build ramparts to protect his artillery. He split his army into the standard left, right, centre and the vanguard and also created a small reserve. His plan was to wait for Ibrahim Lodi to attack the fortified line and then have his flanking parties, known as Tulghama contingents, attack the enemie's rear. He wanted Lodi to attack first so that his field artillery could have the most devastating effect and play havoc as the Hindustani's had not seen any thing like it before.

For one week before the battle, the two forces just faced each other. Babur tried provoking Ibrahim Lodi into attacking from the front. Every day, his archers would sally out towards the enemy camp and fire arrows into their massed ranks. But Ibrahim Lodi ignored this provocation. In desperation, Babur launched a small attack in the evening, just at sunset. He attacked from the side of the setting sun so that the enemy could not accurately make out the number of attackers in the glare of the setting sun. The attack lasted till night fell. Babur pretended that Ibrahim Lodi's forces had managed to repulse his men, who pretended to retreat in disarray. Unfortunately, in the darkness, his men got lost and the morning found them in a very vulnerable position in no man's land very near the enemy. Babur sent Humayun to the help of his stranded men and followed with his entire army. In the skirmish that followed, some of Ibrahim Lodi's men and officers were captured. Babur sent a contemptuous challenge through one of the officers, calling Ibrahim Lodi a coward who would not attack because he was scared, weak and spineless. This did the trick and acted as the provocation that Babur was trying for.

Finally, on April 21, Ibrahim Lodi attacked. Most of Ibrahim Lodi's army was neither well uniformed nor well equipped. Most of the infantry was dressed in only loin cloths and carried only spears to fight with.

In a pincer movement, Babur's flanking parties attacked the rear of the forces of Ibrahim Lodi. Simultaneously, his left and right wings attacked the sides of Ibrahim Lodi's forces. Having surrounded the enemy, Babur's archers created mayhem. The battle lasted from morning till late noon. According to *Babur Nama* (Babur's memoirs), Babur's men killed 15,000-16,000 of the enemy, although according to the people of Agra, 40,000-

50,000 died. Many others were captured. Ibrahim Lodi was killed by an arrow that went through his throat. His army was routed. Babur sent Humayun after the fleeing soldiers and men of Ibrahim Lodi to kill them or take them prisoner and prevent them from regrouping and taking a stand somewhere else. It is said that it was during this chase that Humayun met a scion of the house of Gwalior who presented him with the famous Koh-i-Noor, the world's biggest flawless diamond of 105.6 metric carats, which now has been cut down to 21.6 gm. This diamond has a chequered history. It was probably mined in the mines of Golconda and was given to Allauddin Khilji in AD 1294. Then, it went to the Tughlak dynasty and from them to the Lodi dynasty. In the beginning, Babur called it "The diamond of Babur", and not Koh-i-Noor.

Babur was joined by Alam Khan, the uncle of Ibrahim Lodi, and Daulat Khan, the governor of Punjab. On the advice of Langar Khan Niazi, he allied himself with Janjua Rajputs, who were known enemies of Ibrahim Lodi. He reminded them of the time when they had allied themselves with his ancestor Timur. He also helped them against their enemies, the Gakhars, in 1521. He gave them high posts in his army, making them generals in his campaign against Rana Sanga. Ibrahim Lodi died on the field abandoned by his officers. His feudatories and generals, mainly mercenaries, joined Babur. This was a pity. What they had not known was that Babur had no reserves. If they had fought on for a few more hours, they would have carried the day. This battle marked the end of the Lodi rule and the beginning of the Mughal rule.

Why did Ibrahim Lodi lose in spite of having a much bigger force than Babur? There are many reasons for it. Babur was a much-liked ruler because he shared all the hardships with his troops. Ibrahim Lodi, on the other hand, was a much-disliked ruler. So much so that it is said that his subjects and nobles invited Babur to invade India. He was betrayed by his own uncle, Alam Khan, who was one of the nobles to invite Babur to invade India. He was also threatened by Rana Sanga of Mewar, who had extended his own kingdom right up to western Uttar Pradesh and threatened Agra. Ibrahim's troops were confused when they were surrounded and squeezed by Babur's Tulghama contingents. Ibrahim Lodi lost control of his men, while Babur retained control of his men.

Babur synthesised firepower-oriented Ottoman battle craft with Uzbek Cavalry techniques. His canons were primitive and likely to burst if used too often, but the frightening sound they produced created psychological terror in the minds of his enemies. He used his armies and his Tulghama troops and archers judiciously.

Three days after the battle, Babur entered Delhi. He treated the family of Ibrahim Lodi well but was only acknowledged the ruler of Punjab, Agra and Delhi. If Babur had lost the First Battle of Panipat, history would have changed. There would have been no Mughal Empire in India, and in all probability, there would never have been a unification of India under any emperor, and Babur would himself have had to go back to Kabul and keep fighting all his life to regain Fergana, Samarkand, etc. There would have been no Taj Mahal or Red Fort and not any of the famous mausoleums. What a loss to the rich heritage of Indian history it would have been. A chapter on a way of life and the rich and delicious Mughlai cuisine, which we all relish so much, would have been missing from our history and life.

References

1. Historyofwar (n.d.). *First Battle of Panipat, 21 April 1526*. Retrieved from http://www.historyofwar.org/articles/battles_panipat_first.html
2. Roy, K. (2004). *India's Historic Battles: From Alexander the Great to Kargil*. Delhi: Permanent Black.
3. Rutherford, A. (2009). *Empire of the Moghul: Babur's Empire*. New York: Thomas Dunne Books, St. Martin's Press.
4. Wikipedia (n.d.). *Baburnama*. Retrieved from http://en.wikipedia.org/wiki/Baburnama
5. Wikipedia (n.d.). *Battle of Panipat (1526)*. Retrieved from http://en.wikipedia.org/wiki/Battle _of_Panipat_(1526)

6

CHAPTER

Battle of Khanwa

The Battle of Khanwa was fought on the 7th of March 1527 near the village of Khanwa, which lies 60 kilometres west of Agra. The two protagonists in this battle were the powerful Mughal emperor Babur and the equally powerful Rajput king Rana Sanga. It was the second major battle fought by Babur on Indian soil, after the First Battle of Panipat in 1526, in which Babur defeated Ibrahim Lodi of the Delhi Sultanate.

Zahir-ud-din Muhammad, known also as Babur, used the title of Padshah. He was born on February 23, 1483, at Andijah in Namungan province, in Fergana Valley in present-day Uzbekistan. He was the eldest son of the ruler of Fergana Valley, Omar Shekh Mirza, and his wife Qutlugh Khanum. Babur, whose name according to Stephen Fredric Dale is derived from the Persian word *babr*, meaning tiger, could trace his lineage from his father's side to Timur and from his mother's side to Changtai Khan, the second son of Genghis Khan.

Rana Sanga, or Maharaj Sangram Singh, was born on the 12th of April 1484. He was the second, or middle, son of the Sisodia, Suryavanshi Raja Rana Raimal of Mewar, in present-day Rajasthan. He ruled from 1509 to 1527. There is an interesting story about how he came to rule. He being the middle son, his elder brother, Prithiraj, was the heir designate. However, a priest prophesied that Prithiraj would not become the ruler but Sangram Singh would rule. This so angered Prithiraj that he drew his sword and attacked Sangram Singh, blinding him in one eye. Sangram Singh, alias Rana Sanga, left

Chittor. Later on, Prithiraj was banished by his angry father from Chittor. Jaimal, the younger brother, was crowned but was killed by his prospective father-in-law. Meanwhile, Prithiraj was also poisoned by his wife's brother for ill treating his sister, and thus there was no one left except for Rana Sanga to assume the throne of Chittor.

Rana Sanga proved an astute ruler who united the various warring Rajput tribes and the feudal lords of Mewar and brought them under his leadership. He crushed Gujarat and conquered Malwa and aspired to conquer Delhi, thus bringing the whole of India under Rajput rule. He was near Agra when he heard of the defeat of Ibrahim Lodi by Babur in the First Battle of Panipat and that Babur had become master of the Delhi Sultanate.

Rana Sanga, from the information he gathered, concluded that with this victory, Babur would now leave India to consolidate his northern territories. He miscalculated Mughal strength and decided to fight the Mughal invader and evict him from Indian soil. He coerced and persuaded fugitive Afghan princes like Mahmod Lodi, son of Ibrahim Lodi, and Hasan Khan Mewattpati of Mewat to join him. He ordered Babur to leave India and sent Silhadi of Raisin as his emissary. Silhadi was bribed and won over by Babur. Silhadi had a large contingent of 30,000 soldiers. He promised to bring them over to Babur's side at the crucial moment.

In the First Battle of Panipat, Rana Sanga had promised to join hands with Babur and help him against Ibrahim Lodi on the condition that after victory, Babur would hand over Kalpi, Dholpur and Biana to the Rana. But during the battle, the Rajputs had done nothing. After he had won the battle, an angry Babur refused to give them the promised places. Rana Sanga took this refusal badly and joined hands with Raja Hasan Khan Mewattpati of Mewat, a Muslim Rajput leader of Meo Muslims. Rana Sanga wanted all the lands around Agra. Although Rana Sanga had sent Silhadi as an emissary for negotiation, Babur realised that the Rana was overconfident of his strength and was anyway going to attack. This time around, the Mughals did not want to fight for any sort of material gains. They just wanted revenge for the way the Rajputs had let them down during the First Battle of Panipat. Babur knew that the forces of the Rana were well prepared and well equipped. He started mobilising his own army to fight these forces.

Raja Hasan Khan Mewattpati started marching towards Biana with 20,000 Muslim Rajput troops. Babur withdrew most of his troops from Agra. He knew he was outnumbered. He sent word to his son Humayun, who was on an expedition to conquer Jaunpur. Humayun abandoned his expedition and hastened to gather more Mughal troops and come to the aid of his father.

Babur tried to influence Hasan Khan to abandon his quest for Biana by releasing his son Nahir Khan, who had been captured during the First Battle of Panipat. Instead of being grateful, Hasan Khan saw this as a weakness in Babur. An angry Babur declared Hasan Khan an apostate, or a person who has abandoned his religion. But Babur was concerned about the 100,000 Muslims and Rajputs advancing towards him.

On February 11, 1527, Babur moved out of Agra but halted a few days later to take account of his troops, artillery guns, baggage trains and camp followers and gather more. He was suspicious of his Afghan and Indian allies and sent them to man his various garrisons. He marched west, towards Madhakur, where he had already got wells dug for water. From here, he went onto Fateh Pur Sikri, which was already considered an oasis and a good place to camp. Still apprehensive, he did not rest here and wait but, very soon, marched out in battle formation. He was joined by Mahdi Khwaja and troops from Biana. These troops had already had a taste of the fierce fighting capabilities of the Rajputs and acknowledged the gallantry and prowess of the Rajputs. The Rajputs were more formidable than either the Afghans or the other Indians so far encountered by the forces of the Changtai Turkish Mughals. They were energetic and chivalrous and loved battle and bloodshed. They were inspired by a strong national spirit and were willing to lay down their lives if required for their honour. They had a hero as their leader. At that moment, they were camped at Bisawer.

Babur gave charge of his advance pickets turn by turn to his officers. When this charge was given to Mir Abdul Aziz, the young man made a disastrous advance towards the enemy camp. The Rajputs got to know about this and sent 4,000 to 5,000 horsemen to intercept him. The forces of Mir Abdul Aziz, which were barely 1,000 to 1,500 in number, were annihilated. Mir Mohib Ali Khalifa, the son of Babur's grand vizier, rushed to help. He found utter chaos. Babur also sent others as fast as they could get ready, including a regular detachment, under Mir Muhammad Ali Khan. Babur mobilised the rest of his army, but the Rajputs, satisfied by their victory in this skirmish, had already gone back to their camp.

Babur had never faced such a huge army as this. At this time, he was joined by a contingent of 500 as reinforcement from Kabul, and he welcomed them. By now, the morale of Babur's army was down in the dumps. Babur refused to allow himself to lose heart. He started thinking that all his setbacks were probably due to his flaunting of the tenets of Islam, mainly drinking of wine, which had been in vogue since the time of Genghis Khan. He had been promising to give this up for a long time but had not got around to it. He vowed to give up drinking wine and called for all the silver and gold goblets and cups. He had them broken and either got all the wine poured onto the ground or had salt thrown into it so that it was undrinkable. He got all the broken cups and goblets melted and given as alms to the poor, the Sufis and the Dervishes. Many of his nobles followed suit. Babur declared, "We have decided to live and fight like the greatest Ghazis of Islam."

More nobles followed suit. An alms house was built at the site where the wine had been poured onto the earth. Babur also gave up the Temgha, or stamp duty, for the Muslims in all the territories under his control and published a *farman*, or declaration, to this effect on February 26.

Babur appointed Mir Mohib Ali Khalifa as his grand vizier. But the morale of his men was still at its nadir. Babur himself never despaired, and to lift the morale of his men, he addressed a speech to the basic religious foundation of the men, regardless of the ethnic or sectarian differences. This speech of his is even today considered one of the best examples of military leadership helping in uplifting the morale of troops. This is a real example of an inspired and inspiring speech if ever there was one.

Babur said, "Noblemen, soldiers! Every man born into the world is subject to dissolution. When we are passed away and gone Allah remains the one and eternal. Whoever sits down to the feast of life must, before it is over, drink the cup of death. He who arrives in this world and it's inn of mortality must know that one day without fail must make his departure from the mansion of sorrow.... How much better then is it to die with honour than to live with infamy." Babur then quoted a few couplets from Firdowsi's *Shahnamah*.

"Give me but fame and if I die I am contented

If fame be mine let death claim my body."

Babur also said, "Allah Almighty has been propitious to us. He has now placed us in such a crisis that if we fall in the field we die the death of martyrs, if we survive we rise victorious, the avengers of his sacred cause. Let us therefore with one accord swear on Allah's Quran that none of us will for a moment think of turning his face from this warfare or shrink from the battle and slaughter that ensue till his soul is separated from his body."

All the men and officers of Babur alike swore upon the Quran and promised to follow this.

On March 12, 1527, Babur finally advanced with his guns, matchlock men and soldiers, now in high spirits. He himself galloped up and down the lines, motivating and inspiring and instructing his men. After about a mile or so, he halted and encamped. The Rajputs heard of this advance, and some of them galloped close to his guns on wheels. But Babur refused to be provoked into a premature attack. After his men had pitched camp, he sent out a few war parties. They engaged the Rajputs and brought back a few heads triumphantly. This lifted the morale of Babur's troops further.

Babur now dug some more trenches a mile ahead of his camp, where he anticipated the encounter to take place. As he advanced to occupy these with his mobile guns, the enemy was sighted. Instantly alert, Babur himself rode up along the ranks, cheerfully assuring his men of victory.

On the battlefield, Babur himself commanded the centre, along with Chin Timur Khan. His right wing was commanded by Humayun, along with Kassim Hussain Khan; his younger son, Hindal Mirza; and Khusrau Shah. His left wing was under Sayyad Mehdi Khwaja, Muhammad Zaman Mirza, Mir Abdul Aziz and Mir Muhammad Ali Khan. Babur's cannons were manned by Turkish commander Ustad Ali Quli, and his matchlock men were under Mustafa Rumi.

Babur drew up his men in a square formation. The front line was protected by the *arabas*, or carts linked together by chains that could be dropped for cavalry and foot soldiers to rush through and mantlets or iron barriers on wheels. He stationed his cannons behind these barriers and his matchlock men besides them. He divided his cavalry into right and left contingents. The command of the cavalry was also divided between his loyal and experienced Mughal warriors.

Babur also kept a strong reserve force, which could rush in wherever help was needed. He also placed two strong columns on the right and the left, known as the *Tulughmas*. These columns, at a given signal, would wheel around the flanks of the enemy in a pincer movement and attack it from the rear. This was a tactic he had learnt the hard way during his various wars with the Uzbeks. He had stationed his Indian allies mainly on the left. His artillery, under Ustad Ali Quli, was stationed in the centre, behind the moveable mantles and *arabas*. His matchlock men were stationed immediately behind the guns, and behind them were hand-picked troops ready to rush out or to repel any attack from the rear. Most of his commanders were veterans who had learnt the art of war under him.

Rana Sanga also had great chieftains fighting under his banner. Silhadi, a Tomar of Northeast Malwa and the chief of Bilsa, bought 30,000 Purabiya soldiers. Raja Hasan Khan Mewattpati of Mewat brought 12,000 men. Rahul Uday Singh Nagai of Dongarpur and Madni Rao of Chanderi brought 10,000 men each. Sultan Mohamud Ghazni, son of Sikander

Lodi, brought 10,000 adventurers; and other chiefs brought any thing from 4,000 to 7,000 troops. There were 500 war elephants also. Also fighting under the banner of Rana Sanga were 7 Rajas, 9 Raos and 104 Rawals/Rawats (or lesser chieftains).

The battle began at about 9.30 in the morning on the 7th of March 1527. The Rajputs made a desperate charge to Babur's right. His reserves rushed in to help. Mustafa Rumi, who commanded the artillery guns on the right, opened fire. As more enemy poured in, more reserves were called up.

The battle on the left was also going on fiercely. After several hours of battle, Babur sent word to his *Tulughma* troops to wheel around the flanks of the enemy and charge from the rear while the guns and the household troops and cavalry that had been stationed behind the *arabas* and cannons advanced. All these movements were carried out simultaneously. Babur's wings also advanced. The roar of the Mughal cannons also spooked the Indian war elephants, who stampeded, trampling their own men. Mounted Mughal archers made repeated flanking charges to the front, right and left. They inflicted the maximum casualties.

The Rajput centre was shaken. The left and right flanks of the Rajputs were squeezed into the centre. Yet, unfazed, many of the gallant Rajputs stuffed themselves into the mouths of the big guns in an attempt to silence them. They made repeated charges towards the centre in an attempt to reach Babur but were repelled. At a crucial moment in the battle, Silhadi, who was married to the daughter of the Rana but who had been coerced into betraying the Rana, reneged and joined Babur with his 30,000 men. This turned the tide of battle and led to the collapse of Rana's forces. By evening, it was clear that the Rajputs had lost the battle at a great cost to themselves. They were forced to retreat through their own dead and wounded, with the enemy after them. Babur chased them with orders to kill and not allow them to reassemble or reorganise.

Raja Hasan Khan Mewattpati, Uday Singh Nagari of Dongerpur, Rai Chandrabhan, Manikchand Chauhan and many other leaders all fell on the battlefield. Sultan Mahmud Lodi fled eastwards and, two years later, fought Babur again in the Battle of Ghagra. A wounded Rana Sanga was rescued by the Rathore contingent from Marwar and taken away. He vowed not to set foot in Chittor until he had defeated Babur. In 1528, he set out to help Medni Rai and fight Babur at Chanderi but fell sick and died in his camp. It is believed he was poisoned by his own nobles, who thought it was sheer hara-kiri to fight Babur.

This battle strengthened the roots of the Mughal Empire in India. If Rana Sanga had won, Babur would, in all probability, have returned to his native land and the Mughal Empire would have never laid any claim to the lands of India. Again, although the Indians had numerical superiority and certainly did not lack in bravery, being some of the fiercest warriors in India, they lacked in strategic planning and coordination. Each man was extremely brave and strong by himself but failed to coordinate with the rest. Hence, Babur, with a much smaller force, proved stronger.

References

1. Wikipedia (n.d.). *Babur*. Retrieved from http://en.wikipedia.org/wiki/Babur
2. Wikipedia (n.d.). *Battle of Khanwa*. Retrieved from http://en.wikipedia.org/wiki/Battle_of_Khanwa
3. Wikipedia (n.d.). *Rana Sanga*. Retrieved from http://en.wikipedia.org/wiki/Rana_Sanga

7
CHAPTER

Battle of Kannauj

The Battle of Kannauj was fought between Babur's eldest son and heir, Humayun, and Sher Shah Suri, an Afghan chieftain of Bihar.

Sher Shah Suri was born in 1486 into a *jagirdar* (landlord) family of Sasaram in Bihar. At the age of 15, he left home and joined the forces of Babur. In 1522, he left Babur and joined the service of Bahar Khan, the governor of Bihar. Sher Shah's birth name was Farid Khan, but he was given the title of Sher Khan by Bahar Khan for showing exemplary courage and gallantry in fighting and killing a tiger single-handed.

Humayun was the eldest son of Babur. He had three legitimate brothers: Kamran, Askari and Hindal. It was while he was roaming around in exile that he met Hamida Bano, the daughter of one of the nobles under Hindal. Knowing that his brother Hindal aspired to the maiden's hand, Humayun still went ahead and married her. Later on, Hamida Banu became the mother of the great Akbar, who was born at Faridkot, while Humayun was still in exile. The story goes that Humayun had nothing but some musk to share around in celebration of the birth of his son and heir, Akbar, and he offered this to all the nobles with him.

Humayun was crowned four days after the death of Babur, on December 30, 1530, at the age of 23. But right from the beginning, his reign was a troubled one. He faced trouble not only from the Afghans and the Rajputs but also from his brothers, who also aspired to the throne of Hindustan.

Humayun and Sher Shah Suri had fought many times before the Battle of Kannauj. Initially, Sher Shah Suri had captured Gaur in Bengal from Humayun. Sher Shah Suri had also been known for using bunkers made out of sandbags in the Battle of Mewat. In the Battle of Chausa, Humayun was hoodwinked by Sher Shah Suri, who at first pretended to retreat and kept prevaricating about giving an answer about whether he was surrendering or not. When the Mughals were relaxed and not on their guard, and when the monsoon set in early, he attacked them in the night and killed almost all of them. Humayun managed to save his life by crossing the river Ganga on an inflated *mushak* (animal skin used for carrying water). When Humayun wanted to reward the *bhisti* (a man who sprinkles water carried in a *mushak* on dusty roads to settle the dust) who had saved his life, the man refused to take any reward. On being pressed, the man expressed the desire to be king for one day. Humayun granted him his wish, and legend goes that he really made the *bhisti* king for one day at Agra. But it was the Battle of Kannauj that proved to be the decisive battle that hammered the last nail in the coffin of the Mughal Empire for the next 15 years. Sher Shah Suri only ruled for five years, dying in 1545 in the fort of Kaliyar in Bundelkhand in an accidental explosion of gunpowder. His son became the ruler, but Humayun only managed to regain his empire in 1555, after Sher Shah's son had also died in 1554.

Humayun was at first defeated at Chunar by Sher Shah Suri. After this battle, Humayun raced back to Agra to consult with his brothers. Kamran offered to fight Sher Shah Suri if he was given 20,000 troops. Humayun did not trust him. Kamran had earlier rebelled and turned against him. Humayun had forgiven him, but there was no guarantee that given the men and weapons, Kamran would not once again turn on him and try to wrest the crown of Hindustan from him. So Kamran went off to Lahore in a huff. Humayun's other brothers also did not support him. Humayun had made them governors of various far-flung provinces. When Humayun sent them messages to send troops to fight under him, they all showed their reluctance to do so. Under one pretext or the other, they either sent just a few troops or none at all. Finally, Humayun fought Sher Shah Suri with 40,000 troops of his own. He had a lot of artillery, but it proved too heavy and cumbersome to take to the front.

Humayun had drawn up his battle lines on a small ridge with dug in trenches. Sher Shah Suri used a pincer movement and attacked both ends of Humayun's forces. When the troops from the centre rushed to help the two flanks, the centre was left weak and Sher Shah Suri launched a major attack there. Sher Shah Suri's army was more mobile and won the day. Humayun just managed to escape with the help of his loyal Rajput allies. He got just enough time to return to Agra ahead of Sher Shah Suri. He had requested his brothers for help, but failing that, he decided to abandon Agra and go to Lahore. He just managed to leave Agra with his women folk and all the treasure they could carry. It broke his heart to evacuate, but he thought it wiser. Some of his troops had already deserted, and some had gone over to Sher Shah Suri. Those left were too few in number to fight against the overwhelming army of Sher Shah Suri. Humayun destroyed the big guns that he could not take with himself so that they did not fall into the hands of Sher Shah Suri.

According to Michael Prawdin, an English historian, this was more than a lost battle; this was a total defeat from which no quick recovery was possible. With all his artillery and war equipment in the hands of Sher Shah Suri, Humayun could not even think of defending his capital or forts. He dared not delay in Agra as Sher Shah Suri had immediately despatched a strong detachment in pursuit of him. He avoided entering the town himself and sent his younger brother Hindal in to collect the valuables and the royal family. But according to others, he did reach Agra and left it after two days.

For the next 15 years, Humayun remained on the run and roamed from place to place, often betrayed by those whom he trusted. His son and heir, Akbar, was born while Humayun was in exile and had reached Umar Kot and taken sanctuary there. The story goes that as he was nearing Umar Kot, Hameda's horse died. No one was willing to lend the heavily pregnant queen a horse to ride. So Humayun gave her his own horse and rode a camel for four miles. On the 25th of October 1542, his son and heir, Akbar, was born in the palace at Umar Kot. Humayun had nothing with which to celebrate the birth of his heir except for some musk, which he shared around with his nobles.

Humayun turned to his brothers in Kandahar and Kabul for help, but they refused to help him. He finally turned to the Shah of Persia, Shah Tahmasp. Kamran, who was ruling Kabul, offered Kandahar to the Shah in exchange for Humayun, dead or alive. The Shah refused. The Shah then asked Humayun to convert from a Sunni to a Shia Muslim in exchange for all the help possible to fight his disloyal brothers. The only thing he wanted in return was Kandahar. Humayun reluctantly, outwardly converted and then, with the help of the Shah, gathered Sindhi and Baluchi tribesmen alongside his Mughal soldiers and first took Kandahar from his brother Aksari. After that, he attacked Kabul. Kamran managed to escape, and, due to his own laxity, Humayun lost Kabul once again and had to fight for it and regain it later.

Still not willing to kill his brothers, Humayun sent Aksari in chains for Haj. Aksari died en route, in the desert near Damascus. His brother Kamran, who had been his bitterest rival, was also imprisoned. Not willing to kill Kamran even though Kamran had betrayed him on many occasions, Humayun had Kamran blinded and put him in chains. He then sent Kamran in chains for Haj. But Kamran too died in 1557, close to Mecca. His youngest brother, Hindal, who had been the most troublesome and active militant amongst his brothers had remained loyal to him to the extent of being put in prison by Kamran for not supporting him in his bid for the throne of Hindustan. Humayun sent Hindal on an expedition that he knew would be fatal, thus effectively removing him from his path also.

Humayun managed to get back his kingdom only when Sher Shah Suri died, but he did not live long to enjoy it. A mild, benevolent, kind and cultivated gentleman, unrivalled in astrology and mathematics, he was a weak king who always forgave his treacherous brothers. He always remembered his father, Babur, saying on his deathbed that he must never do anything against his brothers, even if they did trouble him.

In 1556, barely a year after he had finally regained his empire, while he was busy viewing the stars from his observatory in a building in today's old fort in Delhi, he heard the call for azan. In his hurry to go down for it, he tripped on the hem of his gown and rolling down the stairs, hit his forehead upon a rough stone. He died three days later. He was buried in the Old Fort at Delhi. But when Hemu attacked Delhi, Humayun's fleeing army exhumed his body and taking it to Kalanaur in Punjab, buried it there. His son, Akbar, was crowned there and became the emperor at the tender age of 13 under the regency of his trusted general Bairam Khan. Later on, his body was again exhumed and brought back to Delhi to be buried in Humayun's Tomb.

If Humayun had not lost the Battle of Khanua and not been forced to run, history would have been different. Humayun was basically a dreamer by nature. In all probability, there would have been peace in India. But he learnt the bitter lesson that in adversity, every one turns against you. The army you have been banking on melts away; the loyalties of the people switch and change. People are reluctant to help or put conditions to giving help. His own brothers plotted and were disloyal to him. Humayun realised that you can never take friendship or even kinship for granted. In the Battle of Chausa, Sher Shah kept mollifying him until he was ready to attack. He attacked treacherously just when the monsoons started so that Humayun's big guns and army got bogged down. The lesson one learns is never take your enemy for granted. Never underestimate the enemy, and always be prepared. Centuries later, we made the same mistake in 1962 during the Chinese aggression and learnt a bitter lesson.

References

1. Mapsofindia (n.d.). *Sher Shah Suri Biography*. Retrieved from http://www.mapsofindia.com/who-is-who/history/sher-shah-suri.html
2. Rutherford, A. (2010). *Empire of the Moghul: Brothers at War*. London: Headline Publishing Group.
3. Sen, P. (n.d.). *Give an Account of the Battle of Kanauj*. Retrieved from http://www.preservearticles.com/2012030925962/give-an-account-on-the-battle-of-kanauj.html
4. Wikipedia (n.d.). *Humayun*. Retrieved from http://en.wikipedia.org/wiki/humayun
5. Wikipedia (n.d.). *Mughal Empire*. Retrieved from http://en.wikipedia.org/wiki/Foundation_of_the_mughal_empire#Early_history

8 CHAPTER The Second Battle of Panipat

The Second Battle of Panipat was fought on November 5, 1556, between the forces of Jalal-ud-din Muhammad Akbar under the guidance of his regent and general, Bairam Khan, and Khan Zaman and Samrat Hem Chandra Vikramaditya, alias Hemu, on the famous battlefield of Panipat, where 30 years earlier, his grandfather Babur had defeated the forces of Ibrahim Lodi in the First Battle of Panipat.

On January 24, 1556, Humayun died in Delhi after falling down the unprotected stairs of his observatory. His son, 13-year-old Akbar, whose original name had been Badru-ud-din, which had later been changed to Jalal-ud-din to protect him from the evil eye, was crowned at Kalanaur on February 14, 1556. At that time, Mughal rule was confined to Kabul, Kandahar, Punjab and parts of Delhi. At the time of Humayun's death, Akbar was campaigning in Kabul with his guardian Bairam Khan.

Samrat Hem Chandra Vikramaditya, also known as Hemchandra Bhargava, alias Hemu, was the Hindu ruler of Delhi. He was born in a Hindu Brahmin family and was the son of Sant Puran Das. He was born on Dushhera, or Vijay Dashmi, in 1501 in the village of Devti Maccheri in Alwar district of Rajasthan, which lies in Rewari in present-day Haryana.

Hemu knew Sanskrit, Hindi, Persian, Arabic and Arithmetic. In his childhood, he was fond of exercising and wrestling. He learnt riding at the village of his friend Sehdev. He was brought up in the religious environment of a devout Hindu priest. He began his carrier as a supplier of cereals, saltpetre (used in gunpowder) and cannons to Sher Shah Suri. He established a cannon foundry at Riwari. For this, he got technical assistance from the Portuguese in Goa.

Very soon, Hemu made himself indispensable and became the right-hand man of Islam Shah, the son of Sher Shah Suri, who had succeeded to the throne after his father's death. He became *shahang-i-bazar*, or the man in charge of all supplies. He then rose to the post of chief of intelligence, or *daroga-i-chowki*. Soon, he became governor of Punjab, when Islam Shah retired to Gwalior for safety reasons. Upon Islam Shah's death, his 12-year-old son, Firoz Khan, was killed by his cousin Adil Shah Suri, who was an indolent pleasure seeker and a drunkard to boot. He appointed Hemu as his chief advisor and prime minister and chief of army. Very soon, Adil Shah lost his sanity and Hemu became de facto ruler. Hemu fought Afghan rebels across north India, from Punjab to Bengal. Hemu had been adviser to Islam Shah, the son of Sher Shah Suri, from 1545 to 1553. Hemu had won 22 battles. He had defeated Akbar and Humayun in the Battle of Delhi also. He assumed the title of Vikramaditya after ascending the throne of Delhi.

At the time of Humayun's death, Hemu had just quelled a rebellion in Bengal, killing the ruler of Bengal, Muhammad Shah. From here, he started a campaign fighting a series of battles in north India. He made it clear that his goal was Delhi.

When Hemu attacked Agra, Akbar's generals fled without offering any resistance. Large areas of Etawa, Kalpi and Agra and areas in present-day Bihar and UP came under Hemu's control. On October 6, 1556, Hemu attacked Delhi and after a fierce battle captured it. After defeating Akbar and Humayun's forces in the Battle of Delhi, Hemu ascended the throne on October 7, 1556. His coronation took place at Purana Quila in Delhi, and the title of Samrat was bestowed upon him. Hemu established a Hindu kingdom in Delhi after 350 years of Muslim rule. He even struck coins bearing his title.

Hemu thought of himself as a native of India. He considered himself a native leading a native army. To him, Akbar was a foreigner, an invader. Hemu's rule itself was secular and nationalistic in nature.

According to Abul Fazl in *Akbar Nama*, Hemu wanted to attack Kabul and was planning to do so. As he advanced in the north, many of his nobles advised Akbar to depart from Kalanaur and take refuge in Kabul, but Bairam Khan vetoed this and decided to attack Hemu instead.

On November 5, 1556, the two armies met on the historic battlefield of Panipat, where 30 years earlier, Akbar's grandfather Babur had defeated Ibrahim Lodi. That battle had come to be known as the First Battle of Panipat. In this, the Second Battle of Panipat, Bairam Khan did not himself take part nor did he allow the teenage emperor to take part in it. He stationed Akbar eight miles away with a loyal and experienced bodyguard of 5,000 soldiers.

In the Second Battle of Panipat, Hemu's army was twice the size of Akbar's army. He is said to have had 1,500 war elephants, and he himself led his army from atop one of these war elephants named Hawai. Akbar's army consisted of 10,000 cavalry, out of which 5,000 were experienced veterans. It was led by Ali Kuli Khan, Sikandar Khan and Abdulla Khan Uzbeg. Hemu led his army in the centre himself. His left was led by his sister's son General Ramaya, and his right was led by Shadi Khan Kakkar. According to Abul Fazl in *Akbar Nama*, "Two armies so collided that they struck fire out of water. You'd say the air was all crimsoned. Their steel had all become solid rubies."

Bairam Khan sent in his ace archers, protected by a circle of swordsmen. These archers held their fire until they were close enough to put an arrow through Hemu's unprotected eyes, which were the only part of his body not protected by armour. Hemu fell. Seeing him fall, his army fell in disarray and was routed. As Badaoni put it, "Suddenly the arrow of death which no shield can ward off struck his (Hemu) squinting eyes so that his brain passed clean out from the cup of his head, and he became unconscious and not to be seen in his howda. Not seeing Hemu in his howda, Hemu's army was in disarray and defeated in the ensuing confusion."

An injured Hemu was captured by Shah Quli Khan, who captured Hemu's prized elephant Hawai and presented it to

Akbar. He also brought the unconscious Hemu to Akbar's tent. Bairam Khan wanted Akbar to slay Hemu, thus establishing his right to the title of Ghazi, or the slayer of a *musrikun* (an idolater), considered enemy of Islam. The story goes that an idealistic Akbar refused to strike a defeated and wounded enemy. All he did was lightly touch Hemu on the head with his sword. Even at that tender age, Akbar had some principles to which he adhered stubbornly. A disgusted and disappointed Bairam Khan took out his own sword and beheaded Hemu, effectively disgracing the young emperor in the eyes of his warriors, who were witness to his squeamishness. Bairam Khan then sent Hemu's head to be displayed in Kabul, where it was hung outside Delhi Darwaza, while the headless body of the ruler was left to rot on a gibbet placed outside Purana Quila in Delhi as a deterrent to all Hindus. Shah Quli Khan, as was the custom then, built a victory pillar of the skulls of those of the enemy who had been captured and slaughtered.

After this victory, Akbar took Agra and Delhi easily, without much resistance. The victory of Akbar in the Second Battle of Panipat, in 1556, was the real restoration of the Mughal dynasty to power in India. It took eight years for Akbar to recover and recapture all the territory that had been held by Hemu up till Bengal.

During the Second Battle of Panipat, Hemu had 1,500 war elephants. When Hemu was felled, Iskandar Khan from Akbar's army chased his retreating army and captured all of the 1,500 war elephants, along with a large portion of the fleeing army. Hemu's wife managed to escape from Delhi with a sizeable amount of treasure. Pir Mohammad Khan chased her but failed to catch her. Hemu's 82-year-old father also escaped to Alwar but was found six months later and beheaded as he refused to convert to Islam. Hemu's supporters built a cenotaph at the site of his beheading, which still exists at the village Saudhapur on Jind Road to Panipat. This battle is one of the turning points of Indian history that established the Mughal rule in India for the next two centuries. Beginning with the Sultanate of Delhi and Punjab, Akbar went on to expand his empire to nearly all corners of Hindustan, right from Kashmir to the Deccan and from Bengal to Afghanistan.

Hemu was the last Hindu ruler of Delhi for many centuries to come. According to historian K.K. Bhardwaj in his book *Hemu: Napolean of Medieval India*, Hemu was a native ruler leading a native Afghan army to victory after victory. Thus, he was popular with both Hindus and Afghans.

A dynamic leader, he was a brilliant tactician. Not only did Hemu believe in looking after his subjects in peace, but just before any war, he distributed *jagirs* and gave treasures to motivate his men.

K.R. Qanungo writes that Hemu's rule was both secular and nationalistic.

According to British historian Michael Bradwin, Hemu's army was five times superior to Akbar's army. It was made up of infantry, cavalry, artillery and war elephants. His generals and soldiers came from various castes and regions and were a mixture of Hindus, Muslims, Rajputs, Afghans, Indian Muslims, Ahirs, Gujars, Jats, Brahmins, Banias, etc. His infantry was run on Portuguese lines. His most noted generals were Ram Chandra (Rammaya) and Shadi Khan Kakkar, who had been the Afghan governor from Sambhal.

According to K.K. Bhardwaj, Hemu's triumphant march from Bihar to Dilli (Delhi) can be equated to the Italian campaign of Napolean. "He came, he saw, he conquered".

Hemu never lost a battle except the last one, in which he died. He won the loyalty of his soldiers by generous distributions of spoils of war. Hemu recruited more Hindus but not at the expense of the Afghans. He also had great experience of administration. He revitalised it and gave new impetus to commerce throughout his kingdom. He was strict and did not encourage black marketing, hoarding or short changing. He came down heavily on corrupt officials, dismissing them.

According to Nirod Bhushan Ray, Hemu was "the harbinger of a new era in which the Hindus were to share equally with the Muhammadans the burdens of state".

Hemu was secular, respected all religions and pledged to rid India of the Mughal invaders and establish Hindu Raj.

John Clark Marshman wrote in 1873, "Hemu was one of the greatest commanders of the age. He was one and all combined in his personality. As a general of sterling qualities he displayed great valour in the battlefield and embarked upon wonderful planning and strategies to win twenty-two battles he waged against the enemies of the state and won all. As an energetic soldier, he never shrank away from the battlefield and when the fight was most fierce, he did not bother for his personal safety and always fought with his adversaries courageously along with his comrades. This earned him goodwill, affection and praise of his entire heterogeneous army consisting of Afghans, Rajputs and various other tribes. He was an outstanding commander and his orders were obeyed by his troops without grudge and demur."

William Erskine has this to say about him: "[I]n spite of the prejudiced and partial representation of the house of Timur, Hemu must have been a man of extraordinary capacity."

In fact, he was such an efficient civil administrator that many appointments of Muqadams and Chaudharies made by him were kept on by Akbar later on. Hemu was on the brink of winning the Second Battle of Panipat when, unfortunately, an arrow pierced his eye, wounding him badly and, thus, depriving his soldiers of their leader. If he had not been wounded, who knows what the outcome of the battle would have been. Probably Akbar would have lost, and the Mughal Empire would never have taken roots in India. This is purely a case of a battle lost because of a chance happening.

References

1. Bhardwaj, K.K. (2000). *Hemu: Napolean of Medieval India*. Mittal Publications
2. Indianetzone (n.d.). *Second Battle of Panipat*. Retrieved from http://www.indianetzone.com/15/second_battle_panipat.htm
3. Mapsofindia (2011). *The Second Battle of Panipat and the Rise of Akbar the Great*. Retrieved from http://blog.mapsofindia.com/india/the-second-battle-of-panipat-and-the-rise-of-akbar-the-great/
4. Roy, K. (2004). *India's Historic Battles: From Alexander the Great to Kargil*. Delhi: Permanent Black.

5. Rutherford, A. (2011). *Empire of the Moghul: Ruler of the World*. London: Headline Publishing Group.
6. Wikipedia (n.d.). *Akbar*. Retrieved from http://en.wikipedia.org/wiki/Akbar_the_Great
7. Wikipedia (n.d.). *Battle of Delhi (1556)*. Retrieved from http://en.wikipedia.org/wiki/Battle_of_Delhi_(1556)
8. Wikipedia (n.d.). *Battle of Panipat (1526)*. Retrieved from http://en.wikipedia.org/wiki/Battle_of_Panipat_(1526)
9. Wikipedia (n.d.). *Hemu*. Retrieved from http://en.wikipedia.org/wiki/Hemu

9
CHAPTER
Battle of Talikota

The Battle of Talikota was fought on the 26th of January 1565 between the Vijayanagar Empire, the biggest Hindu empire at that time in southern India, and the Deccan Sultanates at Talikota in northern Karnataka, about 80 kilometres southeast of Bijapur city.

The Vijayanagar Empire got its name from the capital city of the same name. The founders of this empire were inspired by Vidyaranya, a saint at the Sringen monastery, and the empire was primarily established to fight the Muslim invasion of southern India. Founded in 1336 by Hariharan I and his brother Bukka Raya I of the Sangama dynasty, it was referred to by the Portuguese as the kingdom of Bishangar. Excavation near present-day Hampi and old ruins there shows that it was a wealthy and powerful empire. At present, it is a world heritage site in Karnatak, India.

The Vijayanagar Empire had a well-functioning administrative legacy from the predecessors, the Hoysala, Kakatiya and Pandya kingdoms. The king was the ultimate authority. He was assisted in administration by *pradhan*s, or what we know as cabinet ministers, headed by a *mahapradhan*, or a prime minister. They had *karyakarthas* or *rayaswamis*, the equivalent of chief secretaries of today, and *adhikaries*, or imperial officers. All high-ranking officers had to undergo compulsory military training.

In the secretariat, there were scribes and officers to keep records and make them official by using wax seal imprints of the king's ring.

Lower down, *goudas*, or wealthy feudal landlords, supervised *karnikas/karnams*, that is, accountants and guards. The palace had 72 departments, or *niyogs*, handling the various facets of its administration. They each had a few female members who were chosen for their youth and beauty. These were trained to handle minor administrative matters and serve the nobility in various capacities as courtesans or concubines.

The empire itself was divided into five *rajyas*, or provinces, each under a *dandanayaka/sandanatha*, or a commander/ governor, who belonged to the royal family. On the battlefield, the army was led by commanders handpicked by the king.

The Vijayanagar Empire was amongst the first Hindu kingdoms to use long-range artillery guns, which were under foreign gunners mainly from Turkistan. The king had a personal army, and there was a feudal army under each of the feudatories. The army was heterogeneous in composition and had men from all classes of society. It consisted of archers, musketeers wearing quilted tunics, swordsmen with shields, armoured horses and war elephants with knives fastened to their tusks.

The economy of the empire was mainly dependent on agriculture. Sorghum (jowar), cotton, pulses and legumes grew in semi-arid areas, while sugarcane, rice and wheat grew in rainy areas. Betel leaves, areca for chewing and coconut were principal cash crops. Turmeric, pepper, cardamom and ginger grew in the remote Malnad region.

The capital city itself had a thriving market in gems, gold and precious stones. Ports like Mangalore, Honavar, Bhatkal, Barkur, Cochin, Cannanore, Machilipatnam and Dharmadam exported rice, millet, pulses and tobacco from Golconda; iron from Machilipatam and diamonds from Kollur to as far off places as China, Java and the Far East.

Though the Hindu caste system was mainly followed, it was a tolerant society. There were many low-caste scholars, like Molla, Kanabadasa, Vermana and Survajna. Sati was common but mainly voluntary and confined to the upper caste. Devadasis and legalised prostitution existed. Women were more liberated.

Exercise, especially in the form of wrestling, was popular. There is even evidence of female wrestlers.

The kings were tolerant. They were staunch Hindus but where court procedure was concerned, they followed Muslim customs.

Aliya Rama Raya, progenitor of the Arvindo dynasty, the fourth, and last, king to hold sway over the Vijayanagar Empire, at that time the de facto ruler of Vijayanagar, was born in 1485. He belonged to the Arvidu dynasty of Vijayanagar. Aliya Rama Raya and his brother Tirumala Deva Raya were both sons-in-law of the Vijayanagar emperor Krishna Deva Raya. The word "aliya" stands for both nephew and son-in-law. Aliya Rama Raya was actually a successful army general as also an able administrator and a tactful diplomat. He had many victorious campaigns to his credit while under the rule of Krishna Deva Raya.

In 1529, when Krishna Deva Raya died, he was succeeded by his brother Achyuta Deva Raya. On Achyuta Deva Raya's death, in 1540, he was succeeded by a minor, Sadashive Raya. Aliya Rama Raya appointed himself guardian and regent. When finally Sadashive came of age, Aliya Rama Raya did not relinquish his powers of regentship. He kept Sadashive a virtual prisoner and ruled in his name.

Aliya Rama Raya was an astute politician. He took advantage of the dissension between the various sultanates of the south to expand his own empire. Again, the sultanates also kept asking him for help against each other as they had helped him to become regent at the death of Achyuta Deva Raya. They kept asking him to intervene and settle disputes. He took full advantage of this, and, like the astute politician he was, he kept changing sides to suit his own convenience and ambitions and to improve his own position. He was what we would today call a *dalbadlu* (a politician who keeps changing sides). At first, he helped Ahmadnagar and Qutb Shah of Golconda against the invasion by Barid Shah of Bidar. He got Raichur Doab for them. Later, in 1549, when Adil Shah of Bijapur and Barid Shah of Bidar declared war on Nizam Shah of Ahmadnagar, Aliya Rama Raya fought on behalf of Nizam Shah of Ahmadnagar. He secured the fort of Kalyana. In 1557, he allied himself with Ali Adil Shah of Bijapur and Barid Shah of Bidar against Ahmadnagar and invaded it.

So the nawabs of these Muslim states in the south were not very happy with Aliya Rama Raya. In the beginning, Ibrahim Qutb Shah Wali of Golconda and Nizam Shah of Ahmadnagar, who were great friends, decided to attack by themselves. They attacked the forces of Tirumala Deva Raya, who thoroughly trounced them. The sultans went rushing back to Adil Shah of Bijapur and asked him to join them. Adil Shah was clever. He realised that they would have to use treachery and surprise if they wanted to win. Aliya Rama Raya was otherwise too strong for them to confront head on. So Nizam Shah and Qutb Shah offered to parley with Aliya Rama Raya while Adil Shah declared that he would remain neutral. Believing them, Aliya Rama Raya delayed his follow-up attack on them, giving the Muslim rulers a chance to regroup.

Sultan Imad Shah of Berar made the first thrust. He attacked the forces of Tirumala Deva Raya, the younger brother of Aliya Rama Raya. Tirumala Deva Raya was guarding the Krishna Ford. In the intense encounter that followed this, Tirumala sent Imad Shah's army fleeing. While the Hindus were busy chasing Imad Shah's army, Nizam Shah, Qutb Shah and Barid Shah on one side and Adil Shah on the other side crossed the Krishna and attacked the main Hindu division.

Aliya Rama Raya was taken completely by surprise, but the good general that he was, although he was old—70 years of age—he personally took over the command of the army and decided to lead it into battle against Nizam Shah's division. Tirumala Deva Raya realised what had happened and hurriedly rejoined his brother on the left flank. He faced the forces of Adil Shah and the forces of the traitorous Hindu Maratha chief Raja Ghorpade. Aliya Rama Raya's second brother, Venkatadri, formed the right wing opposite Qutb Shah and Barid Shah, who were reinforced by Nizam Shah's auxiliaries as the battle progressed.

On January 23, 1565, the two enormous armies clashed on the plains near the villages of Rakshasi and Tangadi. Some historians claim that more than a million men were involved in the clash. Venkatadri struck early. In the first two hours, the guns of the Hindu right wing fired constantly on the ranks of Barid Shah. As the rank and file were devastated and softened, Venkatadri led his men in a charge annihilating the enemy as he and his men literally ploughed through them. This charge was so fierce that a Hindu victory was almost certain. Qutb Shah had also been forced to retreat. Nizam Shah was hardpressed as Aliya Rama Raya led an infantry assault against him himself. At this time, Nizam Shah signalled to the Muslim officers in Aliya Rama Raya's army. Suddenly, Aliya Rama Raya found that two of his Muslim divisions that were in his rear had turned against him. Approximately, 140,000 Muslim troops attacked his forces from the rear. They captured several artillery positions along with the cannons. Cannon shells started landing near the elephant Aliya Rama Raya was riding. Aliya Rama Raya fell down. Nizam Shah raced towards him to capture him.

Aliya Rama Raya was captured and dragged to the Muslim camp. Nizam Shah asked him to acknowledge Allah. Aliya Rama Raya refused and instead yelled, "Narayan Krishna Bhagwanta!" Nizam Shah was so angry that he immediately took out his sword and slit Aliya Rama Raya's throat and declared himself a ghazi, or the killer of a kafir, or unbeliever. Aliya Rama Raya's head was put on a pole and waved in front of the Hindu troops, demoralising them. They lost heart, and panic ensued. Venkatadri and the Hindu's were routed.

Qutb Shah, Barid Shah and Nizam Shah joined forces and attacked Tirumala. Tirumal tried to hold on in the middle, but Adil Shah's division made a final assault from the rear. Vijayanagar's artillery was exhausted by now. Adil Shah's artillery blasted them, and the Hindu's were routed.

Tirumala Deva Raya fled to Vijayanagar. When the people of Vijayanagar saw him entering the city with a dejected expression upon his face, they feared the worst. Tirumala only waited long enough to pick up the treasury, and along with the puppet king and 1,500 elephants, fled south, to Penukonda.

The news of Vijayanagar's defeat spread like wildfire. The troops of the nawabs camped outside the town for three days. Meanwhile, brigands and decoits, under Raja Ghorpade Bahadur and Maharashtrian Brahmin Murari Rao, entered and looted the city. Even after the nawab's men had entered the city, looting went on for the next six months. After this, the sultans' men put the city to the torch and burnt it down. According to some historians, the heat from the burning city was so intense that it left cracks in the surrounding granite hills.

It is said that Aliya Rama Raya's skull was taken by Nizam Shah to Ahmadnagar and fitted onto the spout of a drain that opened out of the fort and was seen there for many years.

What were the causes of the defeat of the Vijayanagar forces? Rama Raya lost in spite of having numerical superiority.

First and foremost, although the Vijayanagar army was numerical superior, the weaponry of the Vijayanagar army was not as sophisticated as that of the army of the sultans. The Vijayanagar army had bows made out of bamboo, while the army of the sultans had metal crossbows whose range was greater and that were more accurate.

The spears used by the Vijayanagar army were barely 7 feet in length, while the spears used by the army of the sultans were 15 feet in length.

Again, the sultans' army used their spears and javelins while riding horses. This gave them a swift and distinct advantage.

The Vijayanagar army had fewer horses and more elephants, which were slow and naturally suffered on the front of swiftness.

All the commanders of the Vijayanagar army were ageing. Aliya Rama Raya himself was 70 years old. The commanders of the sultans' army were young in comparison.

The sultans' army had better artillery, managed by Turks, the originator of the big guns. Aliya Rama Raya depended upon mercenary European gunners, who were not so well trained nor so efficient.

Again, Vijayanagar had generated a lot of ill-will in the neighbouring kingdoms by pillaging and warring with them. So they had to stand alone when they were attacked.

The nepotism of Aliya Rama Raya and his brother in appointing incompetent relatives to high posts backfired as this led to civil unrest. So they did not even have the support of their own population at the time of the crisis.

Aliya Rama Raya was betrayed by his two Muslim divisions at the crucial moment. This resulted in chaos and led to the rout of his army. The officers of the Muslim divisions had been called secretly a day before by the sultans and their associates, and they had been persuaded to betray Aliya Rama Raya at the crucial juncture when they were needed.

There was a total failure of Aliya Rama Raya's intelligence service, which was a major cause of the loss. He had no inkling about the subversion of his Muslim officers.

Rama Raya was killed, and Tirumala Deva Raya and Venkatadri fled.

The army of the sultans waited outside the gates of Vijayanagar for three days before entering. In these three days, Vijayanagar was looted and destroyed. When the army entered, it looted further and then torched the city.

Robert Sewell, in his book *A Forgotten Empire: Vijayanagar*, says, "With fire and sword, with crowbar and axes, they carried on day after day their work of destruction. Never perhaps in history of the world has such havoc been wrought and wrought so suddenly, on so splendid a city teeming with a wealthy and industrious population in the full of plenitude of prosperity one day, and on the next seized, pillaged and reduced to ruins and scenes of savage massacre and horror begging description...."

References

1. Wikipedia (n.d.). *Aliya Rama Raya*. Retrieved from http://en.wikipedia.org/wiki/Aliya_Rama_Raya
2. Wikipedia (n.d.). *Battle of Talikota*. Retrieved from http//en.wikipedia.org/wiki/Battle_of_Talikota
3. Wikipedia (n.d.). *Vijayanagara Empire*. Retrieved from http://en.wikipedia.org/wiki/Vijayanagar_empire

10 CHAPTER

Battle of Haldighati

The Battle of Haldighati was fought between Maharana Pratap of Mewar and the Mughal emperor Akbar on June 21, 1576. It holds a unique place in the annals of our history. It was like the proverbial confrontation between David and Goliath. The two protagonists were each in their own way giants of their times. One held sway over nearly the whole of India, while the other refused to pay abeyance to him, preferring a hard life on the run to being a pampered puppet of the great emperor. He was a man not after power or riches but a man with a mission in life. He was considered the raja of all of Rajputana, except Chittor. He refused to be crowned until he had won Chittor back from the Mughals. The conflict between him and Akbar had its roots probably in the bitter rivalry that had raged between the grandfathers of the two men, namely Babur and Rana Sanga, who had struggled and fought over the Gangetic plain and the Doab, the region between the Ganga and the Jamuna.

Akbar was very young when his father, Humayun, while going to answer the call for prayer, slipped down some stairs and died. One of his favoured ministers Bairam Khan took the reigns of the kingdom in his hands and acted as regent for the young Akbar. In 1559, Akbar sent Bairam Khan on a pilgrimage to Mecca and, it is said, he had him killed on the way. By 1572, Akbar had conquered a large part of India. He was a shrewd and intelligent ruler. He abolished the distinction between the Hindus and the Muslims, and his policy of *mansabdari* facilitated him a lot. He made many alliances with Hindu kings by marrying their daughters.

Akbar organised his army well and also his civil administration. He had a standing army of 25,000 soldiers, while the contingents of the *mansabdars* could swell this to any number.

Akbar controlled the chiefs who had surrendered to him by forcing them to give up all their possessions to him and then he would return their possessions to them as *jagirs*. He made them either stay at his court themselves or leave their eldest sons there as their representatives. After a chieftain died, Akbar acknowledged the heir by conferring an imperial *sannad* upon him. By doing this, he reserved the right to choose the successor.

But the Battle of Haldighati was mainly between Maharana Pratap and Akbar's representative Raja Maan Singh, the Kuchwaha king of Amber, the modern-day Jaipur. Maan Singh was the son of Raja Bhagwant and Rani Sa Bhagwati Ji of Amber. He was 10 years younger than Maharana Pratap. He was one of the nine gems of Akbar's court, and his grandfather had been the first Rajput king to give his daughter in marriage to the Mughals. He was also the trusted general of Akbar. Maharana Pratap was born on May 9, 1540, to Rana Udai Singh of Mewar. Although he was the eldest son, Udai Singh did not want him to succeed him; instead, he wanted his second son, Jagmal, from his favourite wife, to succeed. But after his death, Pratap's maternal uncle Rao Akhai, Raja of Jhalor, along with Rawat Kishan Dass, Rawat Sanga and Raja Ram Prasad, the deprived ruler of Gwalior, convinced Pratap that Jagmal was not a fit ruler and decided upon a *coup de main*. They forced Jagmal to vacate the throne and placed Pratap upon it. Jagmal deserted to the Mughals and went over to Akbar's court, where he was granted the *jagir* of Jahajpur, the modern Mewar. In fact, two other brothers of Rana Pratap, Shakti Singh and Pratap Singh, also went over to serve under Akbar.

The factors and events that led up to the famous Battle of Haldighati were numerous. Udai Singh had always considered the Mughals as invaders. He called Akbar "a Turk" and not an emperor. Akbar had the policy of gaining territory by conquering it and then consolidating it by strengthening the tie by marrying into the royal family of that place. Many Rajput clans had acknowledged his suzerainty by marrying one of their daughters to Akbar. Pratap was one of the few rajas who refused to bow down to the might of Akbar. He preferred his freedom. Akbar sent a total of six diplomatic missions to Rana Pratap, but all of them failed. He even sent Raja Maan Singh to try and lure Pratap. Raja Maan Singh decided to visit Pratap as a Rajput instead of an emissary of Akbar. Pratap was courteous to him but refused to eat food with him, pretending an indisposition, thus insulting Maan Singh, who became his bitter enemy. Maan Singh never forgave Maharana Pratap for the insult.

Akbar also tried to lure Maharana Pratap by sending Raja Bhagwan Das as an emissary after Maan Singh had failed. But Bhagwan Das also failed.

Thus, Akbar was forced to attack and fight Maharana Pratap in an attempt to bring him to heel.

Maharana Pratap was a brave and chivalrous man. He had 114 ranis. He had vowed that until he took Chittor, which he had been forced to leave, he would sleep on the floor in a hut. After his death, on January 19, 1597, at Chavinda, his son Amar Singh carried on the fight and fought 17 battles against the Mughals, until he was forced to give in but, in the end accepted, Akbar's suzerainty conditionally.

There are many tales of Maharana Pratap's chivalry that till today are told and sung about in that area. Once, before the Battle of Haldighati, Raja Maan Singh had gone out hunting with a small contingent of just 100 or 200 men. Maharana Pratap got to know this through his Bhil spies. His nobles wanted him to attack Maan Singh and kill him, but Maharana Pratap refused to do so.

Another time, the women folk of Abdur Rahim Khankhana and a Mughal officer escorting them fell into the hands of Maharana's son Amar Singh. At that time, Khankhana was on his way to fight the Maharana and was camping at Sherpur, making preparations for the encounter. Maharana Pratap commanded his son to return the ladies to the camp of Khankhana with dignity and respect. Khankhana was so impressed that he later refused to fight the Maharana.

On April 3, 1576, Akbar sent Kanwar Maan Singh, along with Asaf Khan, the adjutant general; Sayyad Hashim Basha; Raju; Sayyad Ahmad Raja; Jagannath Kachwaha, the uncle of Maan Singh; Mehtar Khan, commander of Ranthambore; and Rai Lun Karan Kachwaha, on an expedition against Maharana Pratap. Maharana Pratap waited for them in his temporary capital Kumbhalgarh.

On the morning of the 18th of June 1576, the Bhils spotted the imperial army crossing the river near Khamnor and assembling near it. The Rajput army moved to the neck of the Haldighati pass.

On June 21, 1576, Maharana Pratap, clad in a chainmail armour and a helmet worn over a white tunic and with his beloved horse Chetak, also clad in flexible chainmail armour, attacked the imperial army at a village called Khamnor just outside the small pass of Haldighati, which got its name from the bright yellow colour of the soil in that area. Maharana Pratap held his sword in one hand and held the ancient banner of Mewar—the golden face of the sun against a crimson background, in his hand. He had about 3,000 Rajput *sawar*s under him, and his 3,000 Bhil followers were under Rao Poonja. He also had some war elephants and a small artillery unit, under Hakim Khan Sur.

The Mughals had 10,000 horsemen, 4,000 of which were Kachwaha Rajputs; 1,000 Hindu were warriors and 5,000 were Uzbeks, Turkis, Sayyads and other Muslims. They also had war elephants and artillery.

Both sides had divided their armies into five wings each. Maharana Pratap's advanced wing was under Hakim Khan Sur, Bhim Singh Dahiya and Ramdas Rathore. His right wing was under Bhamashah and Ramshaha Tanwar. His left wing was under Jhala Maan Singh. Maharana Pratap himself was commanding the centre. Behind him was Rao Poonja with the Bhil warriors.

The Mughals had two advanced wings. The first of these was under Sayyad Hashim Barahs, Barah Jagannath Kachwaha and Asif Ali Khan. The second was headed by Madho Singh Kachwaha. Behind these was Maan Singh. To his right was Mulla Kazikhan Badkhsi, and to his left were the Sayyads of Barah.

For the first time, the Rajputs took the offensive. They emerged from the pass and attacked the advance wings and the left wings of the Mughals and scattered them by the very fierceness of their attack. Jagannath Kachwaha was killed. Under Ramesh Tanwer, the Rajputs fought fiercely. The Mughals could not distinguish between their own men and the enemy and indiscriminately killed many Rajput warriors from both sides. The battle raged all day, and the Rajputs fought so fiercely that they nearly carried the day. The imperial army was routed and was running away when Mehtar Khan, who was in reserve, jumped into the fray. He stopped the flight of the imperial soldiers by making them believe that the emperor himself was coming to their aid. The fleeing soldiers stopped and rallied once again. The exhausted Rajputs started falling. Maharana Pratap had made his way to where Maan Singh sat atop his elephant. His brave horse, Chetak, put his front hooves on the trunk of the elephant, and the Maharana threw his lance. This lance killed the mahout and cut the traces of the howdah, which came crashing down, throwing Maan Singh into the dust. But he hid, and meanwhile the Maharana was surrounded. Bahlol Khan charged at him to kill him, but the Maharana fought his way through to his own men. Chetak had been injured by the elephant's sword, but he managed to carry his master to safety. Suddenly, there was the beat of the victory drums. The Rajput warriors panicked. Maharana Pratap would have been killed but for one of his generals, Mana Jhala, who snatched the crown and the Sisodia standard from him and drew all the attack upon himself, thus allowing Maharana Pratap to escape. Mana Jhala was killed soon afterwards. Maharana Pratap was chased by two Mughals but was saved by his brother Sakta.

The battle ended after seven hours, and although the Rajputs withdrew, the imperial army did not pursue them. It is difficult to decide who won as there were no clear results. The casualties on both sides were heavy, but the main protagonists escaped barely by the skin of their teeth and by the stratagems of their subordinates, namely Mehtar Khan and Mana Jhala. The Rajputs declared this as their victory, while Akbar's forces did the same. According to historical accounts, nearly 18,000 soldiers were killed from both sides. The battlefield turned into a lake of blood as rain poured down in the afternoon. The place where this battle took place is known as Rakt Talai (lake of blood).

Chetak, having carried his master to safety, collapsed while jumping over a small brook a few kilometres away from the battlefield. A famous couplet narrates this incident very aptly.

> "*Aage nadia padi apaar, kaise utare paar Raane socha is paar, tab tak chetak tha us paar.*"

(Lies the boundless river ahead. How will the horse cross it? While Rana thought on his side, Chetak had reached that side.)

A monument to the loyal, brave horse stands at the site where he fell.

The Battle of Haldighati strengthened the resolve of the Rajputs to carry on the ceaseless guerrilla warfare. It gave them fresh confidence in their own strength. They became bolder.

Maharana Pratap, with the help of the money donated by a trader Bhama Shah, continued his war against Akbar and was a thorn in Akbar's side till he died on January 19, 1597. He was cremated on the banks of a stream near the village of Badeli, where his cenotaph still exists. On his deathbed, he made his son Amar Singh take an oath to continue the war against the Mughals. Amar Singh fought 17 battles against the Mughals but in the end, during the reign of Emperor Jahangir, accepted their rule conditionally.

There were many lessons learnt from this battle. Some of them are as follows:

- It is of paramount importance to meet an enemy at a place of your choosing and at the time of your choice.
- The enemy's supply lines must be cut to weaken the enemy.

- Subterfuge must be used to confuse the enemy into believing that your strength is much more than it really is. Rommel used this tactic to great advantage against the Allied forces during the desert warfare in north Africa during World War II.
- Psychological warfare can turn a defeat into a victory if used properly, at the right time and with the right amount of cunning, for example, when Mehtar Khan convinced the Mughal army to fight on with the assurance that Akbar himself was coming to its aid and also when Mana Jhala allowed Maharana Pratap to escape by snatching his crown and standard and getting the enemy to believe that he was the Rana.

References

1. *Battle of Haldighati* (18th June 1576) (n.d.). Retrieved from https://sites.google.com/site/airavat/battleofhaldighati
2. Echarcha (2005). *History: The War of Haldighati.* Retrieved from http://www.echarcha.com/forum/showthread.php?t=19959
3. Wikipedia (n.d.). *Maharana Pratap.* Retrieved from http://en.wikipedia.org/wiki/Maharana_Pratap

11 CHAPTER

Battle of Samugarh

This was the decisive battle fought between three of the sons of Shah Jahan after he took ill in 1657. It was fought between Dara Shikoh, the heir apparent, and his two younger brothers, Aurangzeb and Murad Buksh.

Dara Shikoh was born on the 20th of March 1615 at Ajmer to Shah Jahan and his third wife, Mumtaz Mahal. He was his father's favourite son and, as was the trend in those days, he got his own command in October 1633, at the early age of 18. On September 10, 1642, Shah Jahan formally proclaimed him his heir, giving him the title of Shahzada-e-Buland Iqbal (prince of high fortune). In 1645, he was made *subedar* of Allahabad and later on promoted to governorship of Gujarat.

With the health of his father failing after the death of Mumtaz Mahal, on August 16, 1652, Dara was made governor of Multan and Kabul. Shah Jahan conferred the title of Shah-e-Buland Iqbal (king of high fortune) upon him on February 15, 1655. By the 16th of September 1657, Dara was commanding 50,000 foot soldiers and 40,000 cavalry and holding a rank equivalent to that of a general today, all without really having proved himself as a commander. He had always been given safe and relatively cushy commands and was actually an intellectual by nature, preferring to spend his time learning about various philosophies and religions, like his ancestor Akbar, rather than learning military strategies.

Aurangzeb, born Abul Muzaffar Muh-ud-din Mohammad Aurangzeb, was born on the 4th of November 1618 and was the third son of Shah Jahan and Mumtaz Mahal. He was also known as Alamgir. Right from childhood, he was different from his languid and laidback brother Dara. Unlike Dara, Aurangzeb was an intense child and a very ambitious child. He did not believe in equality of religions and tended to be puritanical in his outlook.

In 1635, Aurangzeb took part in the siege of Orchha. He became viceroy of the Deccan in 1636. He brought the Nizam Shah dynasty of Ahmadnagar to an end. He conquered the small kingdom of Baglana in 1637. In 1644, his elder sister Jahanara got burnt when her clothes caught fire from a lamp in the corridors of the palace. Instead of returning immediately to see her, Aurangzeb put in an appearance after three whole weeks. This angered Shah Jahan, who dismissed him as viceroy of the Deccan. He also stripped Aurangzeb of privileges like being allowed to use a crimson royal tent, etc. These were instead given to Dara. In 1645, Aurangzeb was barred from court for seven months. This led to a lot of resentment as Aurangzeb blamed Dara for manipulating things at the court of his father for his own ends, thus leading to the disgrace of Aurangzeb.

Aurangzeb was sent back to the Deccan as the governor. The Deccan was a relatively poor province, and Aurangzeb suffered financially. Shah Jahan was of the opinion that Aurangzeb could enrich the Deccan by implementing agricultural reforms, but Aurangzeb did not work hard enough or really care to do so. What Shah Jahan did not realise was that agricultural reforms take time to implement. This led to a lot of bad blood between father and son.

Again, when Aurangzeb attacked Golconda and Bijapur, the former under the Qutb Shahi rulers and the latter under Adil Shahi rulers, at the last moment, when he was about to go in for the kill, Shah Jahan decided to negotiate with them. Thus, Aurangzeb was robbed of a complete victory and had to be satisfied with a nominal acknowledgement of suzerainty instead of total enslavement. Aurangzeb felt cheated and again blamed this on Dara.

According to historians, all four sons of Shah Jahan were contenders for the throne as Muslims have no tradition of primogeniture (eldest son inheriting the throne), and each of them had held the post of governor of some province or the other, but Aurangzeb and Dara were the main contenders.

Dara was an intellectual and a religious liberal in the mould of his ancestor Akbar. Aurangzeb was much more conservative, puritanical and fanatical in his outlook. Dara had always had safe and cushy commands and, thus, had never really been put to the test; he was a poor leader and general. He took his succession to the throne for granted. Aurangzeb had seen a tougher life, did not take his succession for granted, was more ambitious and was definitely a better commander.

When Shah Jahan fell ill with stranguary in 1657 at Shahjahanabad (Old Delhi), he nominated Dara as his heir. Rumours of Shah Jahan's death spread rapidly, and each of his three sons who were not near him prepared to battle for the throne. Shah Suja was in Bengal, Aurangzeb was in the Deccan and Murad was in Gujarat. Each of them proclaimed himself emperor in his own state.

Shah Suja was defeated at Benaras in February 1658 by the forces of Shah Jahan, under the command of Dara's son Sulaiman Shikoh, who chased Shah Suja. Murad and Aurangzeb ganged up together. Murad had always been in awe of Aurangzeb, and Aurangzeb persuaded him to join up with him. They agreed to split the empire between them once they had won.

After the rumours of death of Shah Jahan spread and when each of the three princes had proclaimed himself king, Aurangzeb and Murad moved towards Agra. They defeated the forces of Shah Jahan, under Jaswant Singh's command, in the Battle of Dharmat. Hearing this, Dara collected fresh troops and marched south to block the route to Agra. He halted at Dhaulpur, built embankments and stationed his heavy artillery guns behind them with his musketeers in trenches behind them. Aurangzeb and Murad were encamped at Gwalior. The road from Gwalior ran through Chambal at Dholpur.

After their victory at Dharmat, more and more local rulers joined Aurangzeb and Murad, including contingents from Malwa. All these rulers were playing it safe by joining the force they thought would ultimately be victorious. One of these local rulers told Aurangzeb about an isolated and not well known ford further down in the east on the river Chambal. The way to this ford lay through thick jungles, and the pathway was rocky. Aurangzeb's forces suffered losses because of this type of terrain, but on May 23, the forces of Aurangzeb crossed over and came out behind the forces of Dara. They started advancing towards Agra behind Dara. Dara was forced to abandon all his elaborate defence works and rush to block his brothers. Unfortunately, in this rush, he had to abandon his heavy artillery. He reached Samgrah and dug in there and waited for help from his son Sulaiman, who was to come up with a reinforcement of 40,000 men. But Sulaiman was busy chasing Shah Suja and failed to turn up in time. This waiting for reinforcement was the first mistake Dara made. It is said that the general who hesitates is lost. A general should attack and not wait. While waiting, Dara's men remained on high alert, thus depleting their energy and strength. They became tired out even before the battle began. On the other hand, Aurangzeb rested his men, and they were fresh when the battle began. Thus, Aurangzeb had won a tactical victory over his brother even before the battle.

Next morning, on the 29th of March, both sides began with artillery firing. Dara overestimated the effect of his artillery fire. Again, he had arranged all his big guns in one single line. Aurangzeb had distributed his guns, giving each contingent some guns.

Some of Dara's ace fighters, the Uzbeks, had already been bribed and corrupted by Aurangzeb. Fighting under Khalilullah Khan, they only made a show of fighting.

Dara's left wing, consisting of the Sayyads under Rustam Khan, made a cavalry charge. This was met by cannonade by the big guns of Aurangzeb, which halted them effectively. The Sayyads veered towards the vanguards of Aurangzeb, who were under the command of Muhammad Sultan. The Sayyads found themselves trapped between the vanguards, the advancing reserves coming up to give support and the charging right wing under Rustam Khan. Rustam Khan and his men were massacred.

Dara had many Rajputs like, the Hadas, the Gaurs, the Rathores and the Sisodias, fighting under him. Without any orders from Aurangzeb, an excited Murad charged the Rajputs facing him and, in his excitement, blocked the path of his own artillery, giving Dara's vanguard a golden opportunity. The Hadas, under Rao Chatrasal, flung themselves at Murad and his men. Aurangzeb's artillery could not fire for fear of killing their own men. Murad lost his chief officer and was himself injured. Meanwhile, some Afghans came up to support Dara's Rajputs.

The victorious Rajputs turned towards the centre, where Aurangzeb was himself leading. Severe hand-to-hand fighting took place. Rao Chatrasal's elephant was wounded. Chatrasal jumped down and mounted a horse while the wounded elephant ran away. All this while, the Rajputs were waiting for some support from their commander Dara. But no support came.

Dara made his second mistake at this juncture. To support the charge of Rustam Khan and his Sayyads, he advanced his centre, thus blocking the line of his own artillery fire. Worse was that the gunners and the foot soldiers, along with some camp followers, turned and started looting Dara's own camp. This was not unusual, and they invariably indulged in it when not watched sternly.

Dara's guns fell silent, while the guns of Aurangzeb kept firing. Hearing of the plight of the Rajputs, Dara urged his elephant and his men to go right across the battlefield to help support them. It was already too late. The Rajputs, in despair, fought bravely. Raja Rup Singh Rathore jumped from his horse, and with his double-edged sword, cut a way to Aurangzeb's elephant. He slashed the legs of the beast and cut the ropes holding the howdah in place. But by now, he was surrounded by Aurangzeb's men. Aurangzeb cried out that the life of such a brave man should be spared, but his men did not hear his voice over the din of the raging battle and had already killed Raja Rup Singh Rathore.

Dara found himself with enemies on his right wing and an advancing vanguard in front of him while Aurangzeb's artillery was causing havoc in his ranks. He got off his elephant and took to a horse. Seeing this, the Uzbeks fled. Seeing them flee, panic set in and the rest of Dara's army also broke up.

The big mistake Dara had made was when he had gone to help the Rajputs. This involved moving his entire centre forward and then swerving to the extreme right. By the time they reached the Rajputs, they were already exhausted without having fought at all.

At this juncture in the battle, suddenly Aurangzeb's band started playing the victory tune. Hearing this and assuming that the battle had been lost, Dara's army fled. Aurangzeb chased Dara relentlessly.

Once Aurangzeb had secured the crown, he reneged on his promise to Murad. He got him arrested and imprisoned at Gwalior fort. He accused Murad of the murder of the diwan of Gujarat and, piously, under Muslim law had him executed on the 4th of December 1661.

Aurangzeb offered the governorship of Bengal to Shah Suja, thus affectively isolating Dara, who was already on the run. Ultimately, Dara was betrayed by one of his own generals, captured and brought to Delhi in chains. Aurangzeb accused him of poisoning the Mughal grand vizier Saadullah Khan and had him executed on the 30th August 1659.

In Bengal, when Shah Suja started becoming too strong, Aurangzeb marched on him and defeated him in the Battle of Khajwa. Shah Suja fled to Arkan (Myanmar) and there was executed by the local rulers.

Aurangzeb imprisoned his father, Shah Jahan, in Agra Fort, where he was looked after by his elder daughter, Jahanara, till he died in 1666, when Jahanara moved into the zenana of Aurangzeb.

The Battle of Samugarh secured the Mughal throne for Aurangzeb but drained the Mughal Empire of all its resources, both monetary and human ones. It also highlighted the fratricidal culture of the Mughals. The Europeans, who were fighting amongst themselves for a toehold in trading with India, realised this and took full advantage of this. They put brother against brother, father against son, and *vice versa*, and fully utilised the policy of divide and rule to their own advantage. Rest is history. They not only brought the Mughal Empire to its knees but also subjugated the entire Indian subcontinent, right up to and including Burma and most of South East Asia.

If Aurangzeb had not come to power and been so ruthless in his policies towards the Hindus, may be the Europeans would have found it harder to subjugate the entire subcontinent. At least they would not have got as much help as they did from disgruntled local rulers who saw in them a better option than the suffocating and unfair rule of Aurangzeb who treated Hindus as second-class citizens and reimposed unfair religious taxes, like the *jazia* upon them, which had been abolished by Akbar.

References

1. Horsesandwords (2006). *The Battle of Samugarh*. Retrieved from http://horsesandswords.blogspot.in/search?q=battle+of+samugarh
2. Wikipedia (n.d.). *Aurangzeb*. Retrieved from http://en.wikipedia.org/wiki/Aurangzeb#rise-to-throne
3. Wikipedia (n.d.). *Battle of Samugarh*. Retrieved from http://en.wikipedia.org/wiki/Battle_of_Samugarh
4. Wikipedia (n.d.). *Dara-Shikoh*. Retrieved from http://en.wikipedia.org/wiki/Dara-Shikoh

12

CHAPTER

Battle of Plassey

The Battle of Plassey was fought in 1757 between the forces of East India Company and Nawab Shiraj-ud-Daulah of Bengal and his French allies. This was the decisive battle that established the company rule in India for the next 100 years. The main protagonists in this battle were Nawab Shiraj-ud-Daulah and Robert Clive, who was commanding the troops of the East India Company.

Palashi is a place in Bengal on the banks of the Bhagirathi River, about 150 km north of Calcutta (now Kolkata) near Murshidabad, which was then the capital of undivided Bengal.

Shiraj-ud-Daulah, born Mirza Muhammad Shiraj-ud-Daulah, was the last independent nawab of undivided Bengal. Born in April 1733 to Zain-ud-Din Ammad Khan (Mirza Muhammad Khan) and Amina Begum, he was from his mother's side the grandson of Aliverdi Khan, the deputy governor of Bihar. As Aliverdi Khan had no successor, he declared Shiraj-ud-Daulah as his successor and brought him up to fulfil this role. When Shiraj-ud-Daulah came to power in April 1756, at the age of 23, he sidetracked his relatives Ghasiti Begum, a rich widow who was championing the cause of another nephew, and Mir Jafar, who was Shiraj-ud-Daulah's granduncle and who had been the dispenser of money in the army.

Shiraj-ud-Daulah also held a grudge against the British. He did not like the fact that they had fortified the defences of Fort William in Calcutta without informing him or taking his permission. They also were misusing the permission granted to them by the Mughals to trade, thus depriving him of lakhs of rupees in taxes. Again, they were giving shelter to his enemies who had cheated him. They interfered in his court and supported his aunt Ghasiti Begum, who wanted another nephew, Shaukat Jung, to become the nawab. They gave shelter to her treasurer's son, who embezzled a lot of money and took shelter in Fort William. When Shiraj-ud-Daulah demanded him back to stand trial, the British refused to give him up.

Major General Robert Clive, the first baron, was born on the 25th of September 1725 at the family estate of Styche near Market Drayton in Soropshire. He was the son of Richard Clive, a part-time lawyer, and Rebecca Clive. The family traced its ancestry to Henry VII. Robert Clive was the eldest of 13 children, 7 sisters and 5 brothers, 6 of whom died in infancy.

Clive, even as a child, had a temper and believed in being daring and devious. As a teenager, he had formed a group that ran a protection racket amongst the traders of Market Dryton, and they vandalised the shops of those who did not pay up. He later on became an eloquent speaker. William Pitt has described one of his speeches in the House of Commons as the most eloquent he had ever heard.

Clive had a very chequered career in India before the Battle of Plassey. He arrived at Fort St. George in Madras (present-day Chennai) in 1744. Already, the Mughal Empire was on the decline after the demise of Aurangzeb. In 1746, Madras was attacked by the French. The British lost, and Clive, with other officers, was taken prisoner. He refused to swear an oath of allegiance to the French and instead, disguising himself as a native, managed to escape with two more officers to Fort St. David at Cuddalore some 80 kilometres south. He helped in its defence and joined the army here as an ensign.

In 1748, he distinguished himself in the siege of Pondicherry. Again, during the siege of Arcot, with only a miniscule number of men at his disposal, he gave such an account of his quick thinking, ability for subterfuge and bravery that he totally confused the bigger army, under Chanda Sahab, who at one time had occupied the throne of Tanjore. Chanda Sahab's army retreated, and Clive got a breather until reinforcement could come up.

Prime Minister William Pitt Sr. describes Clive, who had received no formal military training, as the "Heaven born general".

After 10 years, Clive left India in 1753, again to return to India as a lieutenant colonel and deputy governor of Fort St. David at Cuddalore.

Shiraj-ud-Daulah captured Calcutta in June 1756 and then captured Fort William. It is here that the infamous incident of the black hole of Calcutta took place. All sorts of rumours abound. However, the fact is that one of his officers put approximately 64 to 69 people in a room meant for 6 or 7 and that had little ventilation and forgot them overnight. The next morning, only 20-23 of the incarcerated emerged alive, with about 43 dead.

It was after this that the British sent a force under Robert Clive and Admiral Charles Watson to recapture Calcutta. Clive led 900 Europeans and 1,500 sepoys, and Watson commanded a naval squadron. The fleet entered the Hooghly River in December. They met fugitives from Calcutta. On December 29, 1756, they captured the fort of Budge Budge. On January 2, 1757, they attacked and recaptured Calcutta. Shiraj-ud-Daulah tried to make terms with Clive and surrendered the control of Calcutta on the 9th of February. After Calcutta, Clive captured the fort at Chandernagar.

On the 12th of June, Clive was joined by Major Kilpatrick at Chandernagar. On the 13th, the combined forces, consisting of 613 Europeans, 171 artillery men, 8 field pieces, 2 howitzers, 91 topasses, 2,100 sepoys and 150 sailors, set out for Murshidabad.

The French sent a contingent to help Shiraj-ud-Daulah against the British. Shiraj-ud-Daulah ordered his army to move to Plassey. They refused to do so until they were paid their back dues. Shiraj-ud-Daulah ultimately, only reached Plassey on the 21st of June. The British forces reached Paltee on the 16th of June. They attacked the garrison, which was abandoned without a fight, and the fort was captured.

The British were outnumbered, but they were cunning. They approached the demoted and disgruntled Mir Jafar and persuaded him to turn traitor. There was a gentlemen's agreement between Mir Jafar and Admiral Watson, Governor Drake, Mr. Watta and Clive. Mir Jafar would be made governor of Bengal, Bihar and Odisha. In exchange, he would pay the East India Company a million pound sterling for its losses in Calcutta and for the cost of its troops; half a million pound to the British living in Calcutta; 200,000 pounds to the native inhabitants and 70,000 pounds to the Armenian merchants of Calcutta. Clive employed Umichand, a rich trader, as a go-between. Umichand was a greedy man and insisted that he would betray Clive if he was not guaranteed 300,000 pounds in the agreement. The devious Clive made up another false agreement and showed it to Umichand. Clive had no intention of honouring this and always intended double-crossing Umichand.

Meanwhile, Shiraj-ud-Daulah had reconciled with Mir Jafar. Clive was hesitant, but Mir Jafar sent word that he would stand by his word to the British.

On June 23, at 1 o'clock in the night, the British occupied a mango grove beyond Plassey, called Laksha Bagh. It was a grove 730 metres by 270 metres enclosed by a ditch and a mud wall. There was a small hunting lodge to the north, on the edge of the Bhagirathi River, which Clive made into his headquarters. The nawab's army had been entrenched for 26 hours before. The nawab's army consisted of 35,000 infantry armed with matchlocks, swords, pikes and rockets; 18,000 cavalry armed with swords and spears; 53 pieces of artillery, which consisted of mostly 32, 24 and 18 pounders; as also a detachment of 50 French artillery men, under de St. Frais, with their own pieces, attacked. On June 23, at daybreak, the nawab's army came out of its entrenchment and started advancing. It encircled Clive's forces, which were much smaller in number. At 8.00 a.m., the battle began, when the French fired the first artillery shot. By 8.30 a.m., the British were forced to retreat and take shelter in the grove.

Unfortunately, later in the day, there was a heavy downpour. The British used tarpaulins to cover their guns and gunpowder. The Indians did nothing. So their gunpowder became wet, and their firing power was reduced drastically.

Mir Mardan Khan, assuming that the British firing power had also reduced like their own, led a cavalry charge. The British countered with heavy grapeshot. Mir Mardan Khan fell, mortally wounded.

There are two versions of what happened after this at Plassey. According to one, Mir Jafar, along with Yar Lutuf Khan, Jagat Seths (Mehtab Chand and Swarup Chand), Omichand and Rai Durlabh, at the last moment, refused to fight. When Shiraj-ud-Daulah asked them to attack, then men refused to move.

Another version says that throughout the battle, Shiraj-ud-Daulah kept to his tent surrounded by sycophants who assured him of his victory. When his dear friend and companion of many campaigns Mir Mardan Khan fell on the battlefield, Shiraj-ud-Daulah was very upset. He approached Mir Jafar for help. He flung his turban at his feet and entreated him to defend it. Mir Jafar agreed. He and Rai Durlabh advised him to retreat behind the encampment for the day. Shiraj-ud-Daulah made the mistake of giving the orders to his troops to stop the battle and retreat to his camps. He himself mounted a camel and with 2,000 cavalry, set off for Murshidabad. At 2.00 p.m., while his army was retreating leaving the French contingent behind unsupported, Mir Jafar sent word to Clive to attack. Robert Clive attacked, putting Shiraj-ud-Daulah's army in disarray and he Shiraj-ud-Daulah the battle. In the British contingent, 22 men were killed and 50 men wounded. Shiraj-ud-Daulah lost 500 men. He just managed to escape by a boat to Patna.

On June 23, Mir Jafar met Clive at Daudpur, where Clive saluted him as the nawab of Bengal. Mir Jafar was told to hasten to Murshidabad to prevent the escape of Shiraj-ud-Daulah. He reached there on the 24th of June. On the 29th, Clive arrived and placed him on the throne.

After his coronation, Mir Jafar, with aid from Jean Law, sent several parties after Shiraj-ud-Daulah. On July 2, Shiraj-ud-

Daulah reached Rajmahal and took shelter in a deserted garden. But he was betrayed to the local military governor, who was the brother of Mir Jafar. He was caught and handed over to the son of Mir Jafar, Miran, who had him killed. Miran had his remains paraded on the streets of Murshidabad. The next morning, the remains were buried at the tomb of Alivardi Khan. In recognition of their help and to compensate them for their losses, Mir Jafar gave the British rupees 22,000,000. Later on, he presented Clive with the quit-rent of the Company lands in and around Calcutta, amounting to an annual annuity of 27,000 pounds for life. In his will, he further left him 70,000 pounds, which Clive devoted to the army.

The Battle of Plassey was mainly won by treachery and subornment of the enemy rather than through fighting. The biggest lesson from this battle is that actual brute strength of an army is significant in winning a battle only to a limit. Other factors, like intelligence, treachery and subornment, can change the outcome of a battle. like they did in Plassey.

References

1. Indianetzone (n.d.). *Battle of Plassey*. Retrieved from http://www.indianetzone.com/15/battle_plassey.htm
2. Wikipedia (n.d.). *Robert Clive*. Retrieved from http://en.wikipedia.org/wiki/Robert_Clive
3. Wikipedia (n.d.). *Siraj-ud-Daulah*. Retrieved from http://en.wikipedia.org/wiki/Siraj-ud-Daulah

13 CHAPTER

Battle of Wandiwash

The Battle of Wandiwash was fought between the French and the British on Indian soil on January 22, 1760. Most people think that it was the Battle of Plassey fought on June 23, 1757, that laid the foundation of the British empire in India, but this is not really so. It was the Battle of Wandiwash, the decisive battle in the Seven Years' War in the south of India that opened the doors leading to the British Raj in India. At Plassey, the French were helping Shiraj-ud-Daulah, the Indian ruler. At Wandiwash, the Marathas and Indian soldiers were helping the French. Robert Clive won the Battle of Plassey by bribing the supporters of Shiraj-ud-Daulah to renege and betray him at the last moment. In the Battle of Wandiwash, the Marathas sat on the fence and waited till the last moment to see which way the dice fell and then abandoned the French to their fate.

It was an odd coincidence that the leaders of both the French and the British forces at Wandiwash were Irish men. The family of the French leader had its origin in Britain, while the family of the British leader originally came over from France. Comte Thomas Arthur-de-Lally was born in 1702 at Romans in Dauphine, France. He was the son of Sir Gerald Lally and Marie Anne de Bressac. Marie Anne's family was a part of the provincial Irish aristocracy. Lally's father, who had originally been named O'Mullays but changed his name latter to Lally, belonged to a prominent family of County Galaway. The O'Mullays were descended from old Gaelic chieftains. After the Jacobite army had surrendered at Limerick in 1691, Sir Gerald had decided to join the other wild geese, as they were known, and followed Patric Sarsfield into exile. Going over to France, he joined the famed Iris Brigade in the army. Thomas Arthur-de-Lally was only seven when he obtained a commission as an ensign in Dillon's Regiment. Five years later saw him doing guard duty in the trenches in Barcelona. Lally advanced fast in the army and by 1774, was commanding his own regiment.

Lally was honest and had his own private wealth, because of which he could not be bribed. He was impetuous and blunt in the extreme, often indulging in savage criticism and sarcasm. Thus, he often put his foot in his mouth, especially where the prevalent caste system in India was concerned, and offended his native troops. He found it difficult to deal with the conniving, unscrupulous and devious ways of working that were prevalent in India and blundered in like a bull in a china shop where diplomacy would have worked.

The commander of the British forces at Wandiwash was Sir Eyre Coote. Born in 1726, he was the eighth son of a clergyman in Kilmallock in County Limerick. His family originally came from France. The first Cootes came over to Ireland in 1600. They were very successful and held high offices in the civil government as well as the army. Eyre Coote was commissioned in Blackeney's regiment in 1745.

In 1755, Eyre Coote was sent to India as commander of a company of reinforcement for 39th Regiment at Fort Saint David. By May 1757, he had been promoted to major and served under Robert Clive in the Battle of Plassey. Clive's secretary describes him as having "a bodily frame of unusual vigour and activity, always awake. Daring, valour and cool reflection strove for mastery. A master at once of human nature and the science of war, his rigid discipline was tempered with an unaffected kindness and consideration for the want of prejudices of those whom he commanded which won him the affections of his European soldiers and made him the idol of his native troops."

In March 1759, Eyre Coote was promoted to colonel and sent to Bengal to command the 84th Regiment. When Clive went back to England, Eyre Coote was made commander of the British forces in India by the East India Company. He was a mere 33 years of age.

Enough about the commanders of the two forces. At the break of the Seven Years' War, in which both the British East India Company and the French Compagnie des Indies Orientales were trying to establish their supremacy in India, Lally was called back to Paris, made a major general and put in command of all the French forces in India.

Lally was personally a brave soldier, but his subordinates were inept and the help desired by him did not reach him in time. It was one of the reasons for his defeat. Lally's naval help was under Comte d'Ache, who was so tardy and indifferent that when just one of his ships developed trouble, he put the entire fleet back to France. When they finally started, the comte loitered on the way, trading in Rio-de-Janeiro. He finally reached Pondicherry in India only on April 28, 1758. If he had not been so tardy, and reached on time, he would have been able to help Lally overcome the small British fleet, under Admiral George Pocock. Before reinforcement could arrive, Lally's officers had rebelled as he publically humiliated them by condemning their misconduct. Then he made the mistake of not dismissing them but allowing them to continue in their posts, giving them an opportunity to do damage and take revenge. Again, he failed to see how much caste system mattered in India and forced the upper-caste men to work side by side with those of the lower caste, causing a lot of resentment amongst his native troops. It was something like during the civil war in America, when the Negroes working for the upper echelons of society in the south were made to work in the fields and they resented it badly. His soldiers also mutinied on arrears of pay.

On November 27, Coote got a walkover in Wandiwash when the French surrendered. Having secured it, he proceeded to Arcot.

Wandiwash, the anglicised name for Vandavasi, was being held by 30 British soldiers and 800 sepoys. Lally retook Wandiwash but was unable to dislodge the British, who were holding the fort. He laid siege to the fort. Lally recalled his second in command, General de Bussy, who at that time was giving a good account of himself against Robert Clive in the Deccan.

Marquis de Bussy was in favour of abandoning the siege and concentrating on the returning army of Coote. But Lally insisted on leaving 150 Europeans along with 3,000 native infantry to continue the siege. This left him with only two French regiments, de Lally and 69th Lorraine, each with just 400 men, plus a battalion of Indians with 700 muskets. He had a naval contingent, a contingent of 200 European cavalry and 1,800 native troops, one-third of whom were mounted. He had 10 light guns and had been joined by the Maratha irregulars, under Yunus Khan.

Coote, on the other hand, had the 84th Regiment and William Draper's regiment; two battalions of East India Company's native troops, one-third of whom were mounted; 80 European cavalrymen; a Swiss commander, de Vassorot; some small field guns and one howitzer.

Both forces were well matched. Only the French were handicapped by low morale and discord. On January 21, 1760, the British sighted Wandiwash once again. Coote got his men to camouflage themselves with twigs and leaves in their helmets and turbans. At sunrise, the two forces faced each other outside Wandiwash.

Coote drew up his men in three lines. Lally formed up his forces in a single line. Coote had the 84th Regiment holding his left front. Two company battalions held the centre while Draper's men held the right front. The guns were located in between the units and on the flanks. The sepoy companies were on the extreme flanks.

Coote's second line consisted of 300 grenadiers in the centre supported by some guns and two groups of 200 men each. The sepoy companies were on each flank.

The third line consisted of 1,250 native horsemen supported and strengthened by de Vassorot's 80 European cavalrymen.

Lally had one of his regiments with its flank in the paddy field at the side. The centre was held by the Battalion of India, and the 69th Lorrain held the right flank. Cannons were located between the formations, with the native infantry behind them. The paddy fields on Lally's left were manned by 200 of the riff-raff who had been dumped on him in the name of help by the naval commander d'Ache. Further back, a water tank was occupied by troops of de Bussy, who was second in command. The French had their horse cavalry and the native cavalry consisting of 400 horsemen on the right flank, to the rear. Fort Wandiwash was about a mile behind and to the left of the French line. The French camp was another mile behind them.

At mid-day, the battle started. Lally perceived some unsteadiness in the British lines and ordered his cavalry to charge Coote's left flank and take it from the rear. But his cavalry refused to move. Lally sacked the commander on the spot and ordered the next in command to do the same. This man also hesitated. In desperation, Lally appealed to the troops directly. Another young man took over command. The attack went well until Coote's artillery with two guns stopped the charge. De Vassorot's 80 horsemen galloped towards the wavering French Hussars, but the men broke and fled back to the camp pursued by the native horsemen.

By 1 o'clock, the British started winning and advanced towards the French position. Lally now formed his 69th Lorrain into a column of 12 and sent them to drive back Coote's 84th Infantry. That unit opened up with platoon force fire at 60 yards. Still, by sheer weight of numbers, Lally's men went through two ranks of the 84th but now were surrounded. Savage hand-to-hand fighting began. Bayonets and musket butts were used freely. Suddenly, the men of the 69th Lorrain had had enough. They broke up and ran as they were routed.

At this time, a lucky shot by the English artillery hit an ammunition cart near the paddy field held by the riff-raff of the navy contingent. It injured 80, including the commander Chevalier de Poele, a knight of Malta. This created panic, and d'Ache's men just ran.

Coote took advantage and sent Draper's men to seize the abandoned paddy field. Meanwhile, de Bussy came on the scene with his men. He rallied two platoons and about 50-60 naval deserters and rushed to help Lally's left flank, which had collapsed. Draper's men reached the paddy fields first. Their guns poured heavy fire upon the French gunners, who ran away, abandoning the French troops and the naval corps to manage for themselves.

Drapper's men had brought two cannons. Now, they started punishing Lally's men. General de Bussy decided that it had to be an all-or-nothing attack now. He charged with his men. His horse got shot from under him. Undaunted, he led the attack on foot. He got three to four bullets. Unfortunately, only about 20 of Lally's men followed him. The others refused. General de Bussy was surrounded and captured.

Meanwhile, Lally was trying to push the native sepoys in the rear forward. They refused to budge. Lally assumed treachery by de Bussy as these were de Bussy's men. The company battalion in the centre just kept firing sporadically and had no heart to advance. The men here were mostly mercenaries who were good when faced with native armies but did not like to fight against whites like themselves.

With the collapse of both flanks of the French and with their centre refusing to advance, the British started advancing.

Meanwhile, the Marathas, under Yunus Khan, stood on a nearby hill, waiting to see which side would win. When they saw the French losing, they just melted away.

In despair, Lally himself took command. Under his command, his European horsemen charged into Coote's sepoy cavalry. Lally took personal command of the Battalion of India, and, joined by retreating troops of his own regiment, they went back to their camp. Here, they destroyed stores and heavy baggage and carried away the lighter baggage. Carrying their wounded, they collected their garrison, which had been besieging Wandiwash, and moved off. They kept Coote's men from chasing them by small-arms fire and some fire from their smaller artillery pieces.

Lally lost 600-800 men—who were killed, wounded or captured—including de Bussy, his second in command. Coote lost 53 from the 84th Regiment, 59 from the East India

Company's regiment and 80 of Draper's men. This regiment was actually the 79th Foot.

Lally withdrew to Pondicherry and waited for a year for re-enforcement and funds or for a peace settlement with the British. But when his supplies were exhausted and he was surrounded, he surrendered on January 15, 1761. A small force of French men held out in the interiors for a month or two, but then they also surrendered.

Lally was sent to Madras and then to Bombay and thence to London. He was treated with respect, but when he heard that the French government was accusing him of treason, he sought permission from the British Government, under William Pitt, to go and fight his case. He was promised a fair hearing, but dirty politics and company officers who wanted a scapegoat for French losses in India plotted against him. He was tried and condemned as a traitor. In May 1766, King Louis XV sentenced him to death. He was beheaded like a common criminal.

Later on, on the petitioning of his son, his case was reopened and the verdict was reversed by Louis XVI and Lally was exonerated.

Lally's son was even helped by his opponent Coote, who wrote to him, "Nobody had a higher idea than I of Gen. Lally, who to my knowledge has struggled against obstacles which I believed unconquerable and has conquered them; nobody at the same time, is more his enemy than I seeing him achieve those triumphs at the prejudice of my nation. There is certainly not a second man in all India who could have managed to keep on foot, for so long a period, an army without pay, and without any kind of assistance."

Coote was knighted in 1771 and ended up as a lieutenant general and died in Madras on April 27, 1783, while preparing to return to England.

The fate of India was decided by this battle as it opened the gates for British domination in the future. It was very succinctly put by a young officer who was inside the fort of Wandiwash during the siege. He wrote that at 7 in the morning, he and his companions heard cannon fire.

"Then followed the battle that gave us India."

References

1. Editors of Encyclopædia Britannica (n.d.). *Battle of Wandiwash*. Enclycopædia Britannica. Retrieved from http://www.britannica.com/EBchecked/topic/635288/Battle-of-Wandiwash
2. Historynet (2006). *Seven Years' War: Battle of Wandiwash*. Retrieved from http://www.historynet.com/seven-years-war-battle-of-wandiwash.htm
3. Wikipedia (n.d.). *Battle of Wandiwash*. Retrieved from http://en.wikipedia.org/wiki/Battle_of_Wandiwash
4. Wikipedia (n.d.). *Eyre Coote (East India Company Officer)*. Retrieved from http://en.wikipedia.org/wiki/Eyre_Coote_(East_India_Company_officer)
5. Wikipedia (n.d.). *Thomas Arthur, Comte de Lally*. Retrieved from http://en.wikipedia.org/wiki/Thomas_Arthur,_comte_de_Lally

14 CHAPTER The Third Battle of Panipat

One of the biggest battles of the 18th century, The Third Battle of Panipat was fought between Ahmad Shah Abdali of the Durrani dynasty and the Marathas under Peshwa Balaji Baji Rao. Fought again in Panipat on the 14th of January 1761, it had the maximum number of casualties on one single day of any war till then. It was the last battle between two indigenous south Asian military powers until the creation of Pakistan in 1947.

Ahmad Shah Durrani was the son of Muhammad Zaman Khan Abdali, governor of Herat and chief of the Abdalis and Zarghuna Alkazai. He was born in 1722 at Herat in present-day Afghanistan and died on October 16, 1772. He was the founder of the Durrani Empire in present-day Afghanistan. In 1729, after the invasion of Nadir Shah, Ahmad Shah and his brother Zulfikar fled to Kandahar. Here, he and his brother were imprisoned inside a fortress by Hussain Hotaki, the Ghilzai ruler of Kandahar. In 1731, Nadir Shah Afshar, ruler of Persia, freed them and gave them high posts in his administration. The Ghilzais were expelled from Kandahar.

Nadir Shah had a soft spot for Ahmad Shah not only because both of them came from Khorasan but also because Ahmad Shah was good looking and came from a noble family background. Ahmad Shah joined the army of the Afsharid kingdom. He rose swiftly to the rank of a commander, commanding 4,000 Abdali Pashtun soldiers. After the death of Nadir Shah Afshar of Persia in June 1747, there were many contenders for the throne. But Ahmad Shah, in spite of being the youngest amongst them, was chosen because of many reasons.

Ahmad Shah was a direct descendant of Sado, the man who established the Saardozi clan, which was the most prominent tribe amongst the Pashtuns at that time.

He was a charismatic leader and a seasoned warrior and had a trained force of several thousand warriors under him.

His main rival, Haji Ajmal Khan of the Mohammed Zais, had already withdrawn.

So Ahmad Shah became the leader. Nadir Shah was the last Afghan Empire. By the time Ahmad Shah invaded India, the Mughal Empire had largely been confined to Delhi and its surroundings. Ahmad Shah and his son, both married Mughal princesses. Ahmad Shah married the sister of the Mughal emperor while his son married the daughter. Ahmad Shah sacked Delhi four times.

On the other hand, after the Mughal-Maratha war from 1686 to 1707, the Mughal Empire was on the decline. The Marathas, under Peshwa Baji Rao 1, took Gujarat and Malwa in 1737. Baji Rao 1 defeated the Mughals on the outskirts of Delhi and captured most of the territory south of Delhi. Balaji Baji Rao, also known as Nana Saheb, was the son of Baji Rao 1 and his first wife, Kashibai. He is mainly known for transforming Pune. The Maratha Empire reached its zenith under his rule.

Balaji Baji Rao had a happy-go-lucky nature, and he loved his pleasures. He introduced changes in the military administration and changed what had been there since the time of Shivaji the great, with disastrous results. He imported Western warfare methods through foreign mercenaries, which cost the army its ethnic and unique national character and affected the discipline of the army. He abandoned his father's ideal of "Hindu-*Pad-Padshahi*", or a Hindu kingdom. He made enemies indiscriminately of both Hindu and Muslim states by imposing taxes forcibly on all principalities south of Delhi. The result was that in the Third Battle of Panipat, he found himself fighting alone against the foreign invaders. He invaded Punjab in 1758. In 1759, he confronted Ahmad Shah Abdali of the Durrani Empire. In 1759, Abdali, with the help of Pashtun tribes, the Rohillas and the Afghans of Doab, defeated the Marathas.

The Marathas responded by sending an army of 40,000 combatants and 20,000 non-combatants under Sadashiv Rao Bhau. They started from Patdur on March 14, 1760, and reached Delhi on August 1, 1760.

Both the Marathas and Ahmad Shah wanted the nawab of Awadh Shuja-ud-Daulah to help them. He decided to join the Afghan. Probably, if he had not done so, the coalition between Ahmad Shah and the Rohillas would have fallen through.

The Marathas reached Delhi in August and conquered it. There were a few skirmishes between the Marathas and the Afghans on the west bank of the Jamuna, which the Marathas won. At this time, Abdali was on the east side of the river with his main force. On the 25th of October, Abdali crossed over at Baghpat and cut off the Marathas from their base at Delhi. The Marathas had holed up in Panipat. Abdali laid siege to Panipat town, which lasted for two months. The Marathas tried to cut off Abdali's line of supplies but were not very successful. By November 1760, the status of provisioning inside Panipat town was miserable. Along with the 30,000 Marathas, there were also a large number of pilgrims stuck inside the town. These families had come to visit the holy shrines at Brindavan and other places. So the Maratha army had to look after them also. All records show that by late December and early January, starvation had set in and cattle and other animals were dying by the thousands. On January 13, the soldiers begged their commander, Sadashiv Rao Bhau, to be allowed to die honourably on the battlefield instead of dishonourably by starvation. On the 14th, after partaking of the last few grains of gram and putting tikas of haldi on their foreheads, they sallied forth to break the siege.

Battle lines were drawn up on the plains outside the town of Panipat. The Maratha line began a little north of Kala Amb. They blocked any movement of Abdali's troops to the north. But their own movement towards the south, to Delhi, was blocked by the line of Abdali's troops. The Marathas had stationed Bhau along with the *peshwa's* son in the centre. The left wing was guarded by troops under Ibrahim Khan. Holkar and Sindhiya commanded the troops on the extreme left. The Maratha line extended for

12 kilometres, with the artillery in front protected by infantry, pikemen, musketeers and bowmen. The cavalry was behind the artillery and bayonet-wielding musketeers. Behind these were 30,000 untrained Maratha soldiers and approximately 30,000 conscripted civilians who had been trapped inside Panipat while on pilgrimage. These included middle-class men, women and children. Behind them was another line of Maratha soldiers to see that no one ran away.

The Afghans formed a similar line a few metres south of today's Sonauli Road. Their left flank was under Najib and his men, and their right flank was controlled by two brigades of Persian troops. Their left centre was under Shuja-ud-Daulah, with 3,000 men. They had 50-60 cannons and about 19,000 mailed Afghan cavalry under Ahmad Shah's vizier Shah Wali. In the right centre stood 15,000 of Rohilla troops under Hafiz Rahmat and other Rohilla chieftains. Pasand Khan covered the left wing with 5,000 cavalry. Barkhurdar Khan and Amir Beg covered the right with 3,000 Rohilla cavalry. Long-range musketeers were also there. As his army moved forward, Ahmad Shah was left behind to observe the battle from a safe vantage point and direct the battle.

At dawn on the 14th, which was the holy day of Makar Sankranti, the Marathas consumed the last of the grains as prasad and, putting tilaks of haldi on their foreheads, came out pushing their heavy artillery guns before them and halted about 2 kilometres from the Afghan line.

The initial attack was led by the Marathas' left flank under Ibrahim Khan against the Rohillas under Shah Pasand Khan. The first salvo fired by the Afghan artillery fell short. The Marathas replied with their heavy guns, but their salvos went over the heads of the Afghans. The first Afghani attack was broken by the Maratha bowmen and pikemen, along with a unit of the Gardi Musketeers stationed near the artillery. The Maratha artillery men readjusted their guns, and the next salvo hit its mark, scattering the Rohillas, who were devastated. They retreated to their lines, and for the next three hours Ibrahim fought on his own. In this phase of the battle, 8,000 Gurdi's and 12,000 Rohillas were killed.

In the second phase of the battle, Bhau himself led a charge against the left-of-centre of the Afghan forces, who were under Vizier Shah Wali Khan. This charge was so fierce that the Afghans scattered. Shah Wali appealed to Shuja-ud-Daulah, but Shuja-ud-Daulah did not budge. This charge by its very ferocity split the Afghan centre into two.

Unfortunately, that day the sun, which had entered its southern orbit or *dakshinayan*, was shining right into the eyes of the Maratha horses, thus blinding them. Again, because of the two-month siege, most of them were starved and already exhausted by the charge, and so they collapsed.

In the final phase, the Marathas, under Scindia, attacked Najib. Najib fought a successful defensive action, halting Scindia. By the afternoon, the Afghans' left front still stood, but their centre was split in two and the right almost destroyed. Ahmad Shah, who was watching from the rear of his troops, called out 15,000 of his reserve troops. He put them in front of his cavalry and musketeers. He also brought out 2,000 light swivel, mounted guns, which could be fired from atop camels. Being fired from a height, their shots went over the heads of his own troops and created havoc in the enemy ranks. He also roused all able-bodied men in his camps and ordered any deserters to be killed on the spot.

These men, along with 4,000 reserve troops, went to the aid of the beleaguered Rohillas on the right. The rest of the 10,000 reserve troops were sent to help Shah Wali, who was still fighting Bhau in the centre. These fresh warriors were all chain-mailed. Whenever they charged, the chief of staff and Najib were directed to attack the flanks in coordination.

With their own men trying to fight these new chargers, the Marathas were unable to reply to the *ghanthurnals*, or the camel-mounted guns. Already, about 7,000 Maratha cavalry and infantry were dead, this even before hand-to-hand fighting started at 2.00 p.m. By 4.00 p.m., against the onslaught of the fresh reserve troops of the Afghans, the tired Maratha infantry started falling back.

Sadashiv Rao Bhau, seeing his men scattering and retreating, got off his elephant to lead the battle. The Maratha soldiers, not seeing their leader upon the elephant, lost heart and started fleeing.

The Gardis, under Ibrahim Khan Gardi, on the left-most flank of the Marathas, were fighting against the Rohillas. Gardi was being helped by an overenthusiastic Vithal Vinchukar, with his 1,500 cavalry, and Damaji Gaikwad, with 2,500 cavalry only armed with swords. The Rohilla musketeers decimated them.

Vishwas Rao, the son of Bhau, was killed by a shot in the head. Bhau and his loyal bodyguards fought till the end. The Maratha leader had not one, not two, but three horses shot from under him. Holkar retreated to Gwalior, where 15,000 Maratha soldiers joined him. Bhau's wife Parwati Bai, who had been assisting him in camp administration, escaped to Puna.

Shuja-ud-Daulah's diwan, Kashi Ram, had 40,000 Maratha prisoners executed the next day of the battle. Mr. Hamilton of the *Bombay Gazette* puts the slaughter to 70,000 in number. Abdali took 22,000 men, women and children as prisoners. These were raped, exchanged or sold as slaves in the markets of Afghanistan.

Siyar-ut-Mutakhirin says, "The unhappy prisoners were paraded in long lines, given a little parched grain and a drink of water and beheaded and the women and children who survived were driven off as slaves—twenty-two-thousand, many of them of the highest rank in the land."

For the next 10 years, the Marathas could not regain their footing in Delhi.

Peshwa Balaji Rao died a broken man. Ibrahim Khan was tortured and executed by the Afghans after he was found performing the rites for Sadashiv Bhau and his son Vishwa Rao. Raja Suraj Mal, who helped the Marathas in the battle against Najib-ud-Daula, was killed in battle.

Ahmad Shah's alliances also did not stand the test of time. Very soon, his allies became disgruntled. His alliances broke over pay and power issues. The Rohillas were given Shikohabad as a reward. Nawab Faiz Ullah Khan was given Jaisalmer, and

Nawab Sadullah Khan Firozabad. But no one was satisfied. Najib Khan was a good ruler, but after his death, the East India Company took over.

There are a few pertinent points about this battle. Why did the Marathas lose it?

They lost the battle because Durrani had numerical superiority in troops. Again, the Maratha guns were heavy and unwieldy. The *gunthurnals* of the Afghans were light and could be mounted upon camels and moved easily; thus they were more mobile and wieldy and created greater havoc.

The Marathas' public relations were bad. They had no good allies. They had alienated both the local rulers and the population by levying heavy taxes. They had offended the Rajputs and the Sikhs by disregarding and neglecting them. They had even aliened the Jats under Raja Suraj Mal.

According to the Sikh historian Kirpal Singh, "Unlike Ahmad Shah Abdali who subsequently raised a cry of jihad, the Marathas couldn't mobilize their resources and make a common cause with the Sikhs in order to pay the Afghan Emperor in his own coin."

Again, the Maratha army was weakened by internal bickering amongst its chiefs. Also, the Maratha army was overburdened with 300,000 pilgrims who were trapped along with them in the siege and for whom they had to take responsibility.

Sadashiv Rao Bhau had no experience of the political or the military situation in the north. The *peshwa* should have appointed either Malharrao Holkar or Raghunath Rao, who were more experienced, as chief. The Marathas had 40,000 combat soldiers and 20,000 camp followers. Raja Suraj Mal advised Bhau against carrying so much excess baggage, but Bhau ignored his advice. So, under siege conditions, the provisions finished faster and Bhau was forced to emerge and fight without waiting for reinforcement.

Bhau's control was weak over his various commanders. Abdali had *harkaras*, or dispatch riders, to inform him as fast as it was possible about the situation on the various fronts of the battle.

The Maratha had heavy guns, more suited to sieges than to a battle. Designed on the Mughal guns, each needed 50 bullocks to drag it into position.

Holkar ran when he could have bought some more time by fighting on.

The last but not least, the intelligence system of the Afghans was much better than that of the Marathas.

The pertinent results of this battle were that after this battle, the Maratha Empire never regained the strong position it had held in north India.

The British started asserting themselves in 1770, and after the three Anglo-Maratha wars (in which the last one, in 1818, was won decisively by the British), the Third Battle of Panipat gave the British an opportunity to step in against the already weakened Marathas.

Nawab Shuja-ud-Daulah ultimately regretted his support to the Afghans and lost himself to the British in the famous Battle of Buxar in 1764.

Najib himself gained but not as much as he would have liked. Abdali refused to give him control of Delhi. After Najib's death in 1770, the Rohillas lost to East India Company.

Some of the lessons learnt from this battle are as follows:

Play to your strength and guard against your weaknesses. The Marathas were specialists in guerrilla warfare. In an open battle, they were at a disadvantage. In an open battle, you have to sustain for a much longer time. If they had held on, probably Abdali would have given up and gone back. He was not known for his patience.

Learn to make friends. They help you in your time of need. The Marathas never tried to make alliances or make them work. So they had to fight alone.

Avoid carrying superfluous excess baggage in the form of camp followers, who become more of a liability than an asset in a crisis.

Last but not least, choose leaders who have knowledge and experience of the area and the population where the battle is going to take place. A leader who is inexperienced and does not know the political and social milieu will be at a disadvantage in preparing for the battle. Bhau was inexperienced, lacking the experience and awareness about the social and political situation in the north. So, in spite of being a brave fighter, he was at a disadvantage and once he had lost his son Vishwas Rao, he had no one else he could rely on and so lost the battle.

References

1. Indianetzone (n.d.). *Balaji Baji Rao, Maratha Emperor*. Retrieved from http://www.indianetzone.com/5/balaji_baji_rao.htm
2. Roy, K. (2004). *India's Historic Battles: From Alexander the Great to Kargil*. Delhi: Permanent Black.
3. Wikipedia (n.d.). *Ahmad Shah Durrani*. Retrieved from http://en.wikipedia.org/wiki/Ahmad_Shah_Durrani
4. Wikipedia (n.d.). *Battle of Panipat (1761)*. Retrieved from http://en.wikipedia.org/wiki/Battle_of_Panipat_(1761)

15

CHAPTER

Battle of Buxar

The Battle of Buxar was fought on October 23, 1764, between the troops of the British East India Company, under Hector Munroe, and an alliance of rulers like Mir Qasim, the nawab of Bengal; Shuja-ud-Daulah, the nawab of Awadh; and the Mughal king Shah Alam II. It was fought at Buxar, which at that time was in Bengal (now it is in Bihar), on the banks of the Ganges, about 130 kilometres east of Patna.

Mir Qasim was the son-in-law of Mir Jafar. He was the nawab of Bengal from 1760 to 1763. Like his father-in-law, he was also installed by the British. Mir Jafar had sided with the British and helped them in the Battle of Plassey. But after he had been installed as the nawab of Bengal by the British East India Company, he had started getting annoyed by the control exercised by the British. He had started conniving with the Dutch. The British defeated the Dutch in the Battle of Chinsura. At the same time, Mir Jafar's army had started revolting as the men had not been paid for quite some time. Mir Qasim connived with Jagat Seth and the British and got Mir Jafar to come out of Calcutta, and then Mir Qasim walked in and proclaimed himself the nawab.

On ascending the throne, Mir Qasim rewarded the British lavishly. To please them and impress them, he robbed and deprived his subjects of land and money. He pillaged the treasury and even reduced the privy purse of Mir Jafar. But, exactly like Mir Jafar, after some time, the yolk of the British started irritating him. He shifted his capital from Murshidabad to Munger in present-day Bihar and raised a personal army to fight against the British.

The second collaborator of the alliance, Shah Alam II, the Mughal emperor, was the son of the murdered Mughal emperor Alamgir II. The eighteenth Mughal emperor, born Abdullah Jalal ud-din Abu'l Muzaffar Ham ud-din Muhammad Ali Gauhar Shah-i-Alam II, he was also known as Ali Gaur. After the Third Battle of Panipat, he had been appointed by Ahmad Shah Durrani. He was the last effective Mughal emperor and was also a poet.

As a prince, he had been kept captive by his minister Imad-al-Mulk and had had to flee Delhi and take refuge with Shuja-ud-Daulah, the nawab of Awadh. He came into conflict with the British when he demanded tribute (tax) from Bihar and Bengal.

The third member of the alliance, Shuja-ud-Daulah, the *subedar* nawab of Awadh, ruled from the 5th of October 1754 to the 26th of January 1775. The son of the grand Mughal vizier Muhammad Muquim Safdarjung, he played a key role in the Third Battle of Panipat. A shrewd tactician, after a lot of debate, he joined the Afghans against the Marathas, even though the Marathas had helped his father before. He was very well respected in the army of Alivardi Khan.

When Prince Ali Gauhar fled from Delhi and took refuge with him, Shuja-ud-Daulah welcomed him with open arms. Ali Gauhar proclaimed himself Shah Alam II while he was with Shuja-ud-Daulah and then recognised Shuja-ud-Daulah as the grand vizier of the Mughal Empire.

The British East India Company fielded 8,000 to 10,000 men, while the alliance had between them 40,000 to 50,000 men. The British East India Company had 857 British soldiers; 5,297 Indian sepoys and 918 Indian cavalry. According to the British, the Indian allies also had Durrani and Rohilla cavalry.

The British troops were under Hector Munroe of Novar in Ross, Scotland. Hector Munroe was the son of Hugh Munroe of Novar. He was commissioned into Loudon's Highlanders in 1747. In 1749, he transferred to the 48th Foot. In 1756, he was promoted to captain in the second battalion, which in 1758 became the 70th Foot. In 1759, he was appointed as major in the newly raised 89th (Highland) Regiment of Foot. He arrived in Bombay in November of 1761. His regiment moved from place to place. Munroe was known for his ruthlessness in implementing discipline and quelled a rebellion near Patnam where he had 20 rebels blown from the mouths of cannons.

The battle of Buxar was doomed from the beginning. The three allies were not compatible, and there was a lot of infighting between them. There was a lack of basic coordination between all three allies, which was responsible for the defeat. Shah Alam II and Shuja-ud-Daulah were at loggerheads right from the beginning. Mir Qasim was reluctant to fight from the first moment, and went off to collect dues.

The alliance's left flank was on the bank of the Ganga, while its right flank was at the village of Buxar. The right wing had, besides the Rohillas, 5,000 Afghan cavalry under Raja Beni Bahadur of Benaras. Shuja himself commanded the right wing. The cavalry in the left wing was under Gulam Qadir and Kuli Khan. Behind the front line, there was some reserve cavalry.

The Company troops were also lined up in two lines. They had several infantry battalions, and each of them had some 3-, 6- and 12-pounder guns. At the extreme ends of the front line were two sepoy regiments. The 26-pounder guns were in the second line. They were guarded by the cavalry of Mir Jafar.

The right flank of the allies was commanded by Mirza Nawaz Khan. It was the first to advance towards the forces of Hector Munroe in the morning. Munroe was ready for them and within 20 minutes had repelled the attack. Fierce fighting followed, but already the Indians had lost heart and the battle was over by midday. Munroe pursued the Mughals. Shuja-ud-Daulah blew up large tumbrils and three massive magazines of gunpowder before he fled, leaving behind 6,000 fellow Mughals and 133 pieces of artillery stranded on the battlefield as he had blown up the boat bridge he had crossed. He had fled, leaving Shah Alam II and some of his own regiments to their own fate.

Mir Qasim also fled with gems worth rupees 3 million and later committed suicide.

Mirza Nazaf Khan tried to reorganise formation around Shah Alam II, but Shah Alam II chose to retreat and later chose to negotiate with the British East India Company.

All in all, in this battle, the British had 1,847 casualties (killed or wounded). The Indians lost 2,000 men, while 4,000 were wounded. The British captured 6,000 Mughals; 133 pieces of artillery and rupees 1 million in cash.

The three allies signed the treaty of Allahabad with the East India Company on August 16, 1765. The most affected by it was Shah Alam II.

By this treaty, Shah Alam II became the pensioner of the British. In this treaty, he conceded and gave the East India Company the rights to collect and manage the revenue of huge tracts of land, almost 100,000,000 acres of real estate, which form the modern states of West Bengal, Odisha, Bihar, Jharkhand and Uttar Pradesh, as also a piece of neighbouring Bangladesh. He also paid a war indemnity of rupees 5 million. The only good thing was that he got back all his prewar possessions except for the districts of Karra and Allahabad. The British granted him a pension of rupees 450,000 per month for the upkeep of horses, a small sepoy contingent, *barkandazis* (matchlock men) and household expenses.

Shuja-ud-Daulah signed the treaty and gave Karra and Allahabad to the British. He had to give rupees 50,000 as war indemnity. The British got the right to trade in Awadh, and both powers promised to come to the aid of each other in case of war with other powers. To pay the British, Shuja-ud-Daulah gave them the fort at Chunnar and later on the districts of Benaras, Gazipur and Allahabad. Shuja-ud-Daulah died on January 26, 1775, at Faizabad, which then was the capital of Awadh. His tomb there is known as the Gulab Bari, or the rose garden.

After this battle, Munroe decided to assist the Marathas, who hated the Mughal Empire and all the nawabs and sultans. The prime victim of this battle was Shah Alam II.

Mir Qasim, who was not a general, was replaced. He also got a small share of the total land revenue, which was initially fixed at rupees 2 million.

The Battle of Buxar and the Treaty of Allahabad, which followed, along with the Battle of Plassey and the Third Battle of Panipat, consolidated the hold of the British on large parts of India. It gave the British East India Company a permanent hold in the rich provinces of Bengal. The British became supreme in the region.

By the treaty of 1752, the Marathas had taken basic control of Mughal *subas* and the right to collect *chauth*, or one-fourth, as revenue. But after their defeat in the Third Battle of Panipat, they withdrew, thus allowing the British free access to step in and take control.

Subsequently, Shuja-ud-Daulah was restored to Awadh with a guarantee of a subsidiary force and defence. Shah Alam II's frontiers were drawn at the boundary of Bihar. Allahabad was returned to him. In return for all these concessions, he had to grant the East India Company the *diwani*, or revenue, of Bengal and Bihar, which so far had been enjoyed by the nawab of Bengal. So now, there was a double government in Bihar and Bengal. The British collected the revenue while the nawab exercised the judicial and police powers. On the face of it, the Company became the revenue agent of the Mughal emperor for Bihar and Bengal.

Even at that time, the British had not thought of administrating the lands they held. The revenue was collected by a company-appointed deputy—Nawab Muhammad Raza Khan. The East India Company had now become the virtual ruler of Bengal and Bihar. In 1793, the nawab had to even hand over the control of judicial administration to the company. So the company's control was virtually complete.

In spite of all the revenue collected, the East India Company was still running into a loss. Warren Hastings was appointed as the governor of Bengal. This was the beginning of the state control of the company. Warren Hastings governed for 13 years. In the two and a half years before the regulating act came into effect, the Indian deputies were replaced by a Board of Revenue at Calcutta and English collectors in the districts. This was the real beginning of British administration in India.

In 1771, the Marathas persuaded Shah Alam II to leave the protection of the British and come under their protection. Maratha regency remained in place in Delhi till their defeat in the Second Anglo-Maratha War, in 1803.

The Battle of Buxar, although short, had a huge effect on the history of India. If the allies had won, the British would have been unable to consolidate their hold in India and the British Raj would in all probability have never come to be. Unfortunately, internal dissensions, and not enough unity, led to the defeat of the allies although they were numerically much superior to the small British force opposing them. The allies had not chosen any decisive leader and thus were actually operating not as one cohesive unit but like three small fragmented units. This led to their route as each one fought just for himself and abandoned the rest to their own fate. Again, unlike the British, they had no designated command structure. If a leader died, there was no one designated to take his place, and thus confusion took place. This was one battle in which firepower triumphed over numerical superiority.

References

1. Editors of Encyclopædia Britannica (n.d.). *Shah Alam II*. Enclycopædia Britannica. Retrieved from http://www.britannica.com/EBchecked/topic/537659/Shah-Alam-II
2. Roy, K. (2004). *India's Historic Battles: From Alexander the Great to Kargil*. Delhi: Permanent Black.
3. Wikipedia (n.d.). *Battle of Buxar*. Retrieved from http://en.wikipedia.org/wiki/battle_of_Buxar
4. Wikipedia (n.d.). *Hector Munroe, 8th of Novar*. Retrieved from http://en.wikipedia.org/wiki/Hector_Munro,_8th_of_Novar
5. Wikipedia (n.d.). *Mir Qaxim*. Retrieved from http://en.wikipedia.org/wiki/Mir_Kasim
6. Wikipedia (n.d.). *Shah Alam II*. Retrieved from http://en.wikipedia.org/wiki/Shah_Alam_II
7. Wikipedia (n.d.). *Shuja-ud-Daula*. Retrieved from http://en.wikipedia.org/wiki/Shuja_ud_Daula

16

CHAPTER

The Mysore Wars

There were four Mysore wars fought in the last three decades of the 18th century between the kingdom of Mysore and the British East India Company.

The First Anglo-Mysore War

The First Anglo-Mysore War lasted from 1766 to 1769 and was fought between Haider Ali, the father of Tipu Sultan, and the British East India Company.

Haider Ali came from humble origins and won favours from the raja of Mysore for his bravery during the siege of Trichinopoly in 1749. Afterwards, he conquered Calicut, Bednor, Kananur, etc. He rose from the ranks and became the *dalwai*, or commander-in-chief, to Krishnaraja Wodeyar. In 1761, he overthrew Khande Rao, founded the Sultanate of Mysore and declared himself the sultan of Mysore. Haider Ali was originally a sepoy in the French army, which explains his attachment to the French.

The British East India Company wanted a passage between Madras and Bengal through the Northern Circars. These territories had been held by the French till 1758. The British applied to the Nizam for permission, and the Nizam refused. Lord Robert Clive then applied to the Mughal emperor Shah Alam II, who in August 1765 granted them the rights to the territory.

Haider Ali felt annoyed with the British because they had rejected his offer of alliance and also because they had established a fortified outpost at Vellore.

The Nizam, who was feeling threatened by Haider Ali, aligned himself with the Marathas' ruling *peshwa* Madhavrao I. He had helped them during one war, and with them he started planning to invade Mysore.

Meanwhile, when the Company started occupying the Circars, the Nizam protested. He would have liked to open hostilities, but he was impoverished and had to negotiate instead. The Company provided the Nizam with two battalions of troops to be used where and when he wanted. In exchange, the Company received four of the five Circars. The fifth was the *jagir* of the Nizam's son, and they were promised that they would get it upon his death. They gave the Nizam rupees 7 lakh also.

The war began in January 1767, when the Marathas invaded north Mysore. They reached as far south as the Tungbhadra River. Haider Ali negotiated for peace and paid them rupees 30 lakh. They withdrew to the north of the Kistna River.

The Nizam began his invasion by March. He advanced as far as Bangalore with two battalions of Company troops under Colonel Joseph Smith. In May, Smith found Haider Ali and the Nizam plotting together and withdrew his men. Haider Ali was supposed to pay rupees 18 lakh to the Nizam to end his invasion, and, in exchange, the Nizam promised to acknowledge Haider Ali's son Tipu as the nawab of Carnatic once they had conquered it.

The two allies, together under the command of Haider Ali, attacked an outpost of the Company at Changama. In spite of the allies having 10 times the number of troops, 70,000 as opposed to 7,000 under Colonel Smith, they were repulsed soundly. Haider Ali retreated to Kaveripattinam and captured it after two days of siege. Colonel Smith retreated from Changama to Trivahnamalai to replenish supplies and men. Haider Ali attacked him and was again repulsed on the 25th of September 1767.

In November 1767, Haider Ali besieged Ambur. He tried to bribe the garrison commander to surrender. The garrison commander refused. A relief column arrived in early December, and Haider Ali was forced to retreat north. He was further disheartened when his entire corps of European Cavalry deserted and joined the British. The campaign failed.

The British started advancing into the Circars and negotiated with the Nizam once again. This led to a split between the Nizam and Haider Ali. The Nizam withdrew to Hyderabad. Haider Ali tried to make peace with the British, but they rebuffed him.

Haider Ali had many other losses to contend with. In the mid-1760s, he had a small fleet of about 10 ships based mainly at Mangalore. They deserted *en masse* as the captains were unhappy with the fleet commander, Lutf Ali Beg, a Mysorian cavalry officer. The British managed to fool Lutf Ali Beg into moving onto Onore and then occupied Mangalore virtually without a fight. Haider Ali did manage to recapture Mangalore later, and he punished the Nair community by levying extra taxes upon them as they had helped the British.

The British took back many places and persuaded the Marathas to join them. A large force, under Morari Rao, joined Colonel Smith at Ooscota in early August 1768. They planned to besiege Bangalore, but Haider Ali rushed back and started harassing the allies. He attacked the Maratha camp at Ooscota but lost heavily.

Haider Ali then tried to negotiate with the British. He offered rupees 10 lakh and other land concessions in exchange for peace, but the British refused. The British wanted much more, including payment to the Nizam.

After many more ding-dong battles, in which both sides used subterfuge, Haider Ali managed to establish control over most of southern Carnatic. He marched towards Madras with some 6,000 handpicked cavalry and some foot soldiers. He was at their doorsteps and as the defence of Madras (present-day Chennai) was very week due to the army being out to fight Haider Ali and the others, the British were forced to negotiate. A treaty was signed on the 29th of March 1769, at Madras, which stated that each would support the other if attacked.

The Second Anglo-Mysore War

The Second Battle of Mysore, fought between 1779 and 1784, was again between Haider Ali and the British East India Company. At that time, there was a war on in America between the British and the French for supremacy. This sparked the war as Haider Ali supported the French. In 1779, Company troops, reinforced by crown troops from Britain and troops from Hanover, which at that time also came under King George III, seized the French port of Mahe. Both France and Britain sent naval squadrons from Europe. Haider Ali was angry as Mahe had been under his protection and was the port through which he got his arms and ammunition from the French; it was important to him. He formed an alliance with the Marathas, the French and the Nizam of Hyderabad against the British.

In July 1780, Haider Ali invaded Carnatic and laid siege to northern Arcot. The British sent a force from Guntur to help the besieged garrison being held by Colonel Munroe. Haider Ali got to know about this and sent a force under his son Tipu Sultan to intercept this force. On the morning of the 10th of September 1780, the British forces, under Colonel Bailey, came under heavy fire at Pollilur. The British were defeated with heavy losses.

Colonel Munroe retreated to Madras, abandoning bag and baggage and dumping his cannons into water tanks at Kanjeevaram.

Haider Ali renewed the siege of Arcot and captured it on the 3rd of November. While he was busy here, the British got the chance of sending reinforcement to Madras under Sir Eyre Coote.

Coote suffered a defeat at Chindambaram but defeated Haider Ali three times: at Port Nova, at Pollilur and at Sholinghur. Tipu, who had been helping his father by besieging Wandiwash, had to lift his siege and besiege Vellore instead.

In November 1781, the British captured the outpost of Nagapatam after a siege of three weeks. Haider Ali realised that an outright win against a superior naval power was impossible.

On the 18th of February 1782, Tipu defeated Colonel Braithwaite at Annagudi, near Tanjore. Both Haider Ali and

Tipu made alliances with Raja Bibi Junumbe II, the ruler of the Muslim Papplic community, and Muslims from Melacca, who were under the Dutch. Already, a war between the British and the Dutch was on.

In 1782, Haider Ali died suddenly of cancer. His son Tipu vowed to carry on the crusade against the British.

A British force under General Mathews took Bednore. But the British supply lines were overstretched, and Tipu besieged Bednore, forcing General Mathews to surrender.

The British captured Mangalore in March 1783, but Tipu recaptured it eventually. Meanwhile, in November, General Stuart's army, under Colonel Fullerton, captured the fortress at Palghartcherry and Coimbatore with little fighting.

By now, fed up of all the fighting, London ordered the Company officials to negotiate with Tipu and end the war. Colonel Fullerton was ordered to give up all his recent acquisitions. Fullerton refused to vacate Palghartcherry on the pretext that Tipu had violated the terms of the ceasefire.

On the 30th of June, Mangalore surrendered to Tipu, having lost half its defenders to starvation and scurvy.

Sir Eyre Coote, the British commander, defeated Haider Ali with a better-equipped and superior army. Tipu Sultan helped his father a lot in this war. He had joined his father at the age of 15 and was trained by French officers. Not only this, but Tipu Sultan and Haider Ali used their French-trained army against the Marathas, the Siren rulers of Malabar, Coorg, Bidnaur, Carnatic and Travancore. At 16, Tipu Sultan commanded a corps of cavalry in the invasion of Carnatic in 1767. Tipu was sent by his father to intercept Colonel Bailey and even defeated the forces of Colonel Bailey in the Battle of Pollilur. The war ended in 1784, with the treaty of Mangalore, in which both sides agreed to restore the other's lands and to go back to the status quo *ante bellum*, that is, go back to what it was before the war. It was just before this war in 1778 that Haider Ali sought the services of Soze Azelais, a Dutch who helped him rebuild his navy. He built 8 ketches with 3 masts and 40 cannons each and 8 smaller dhows for Haider Ali. During the first and second

Mysore wars, Haider Ali came within striking distance of the port of Madras but never conquered or annexed it. It was at the end of this war that for the last time any Indian king dictated terms to the British, who were under orders from London to cooperate.

The Third Anglo-Mysore War

The Third Anglo-Mysore War was fought between East India Company and its allies the Marathas on one side and the Nizam of Hyderabad and Tipu Sultan on the other. It lasted from 1789 to 1790.

Tipu Sultan was born in November 1750 in Budikot at a place called Devanahali, which lies some 33 kilometres north of present-day Bengaluru city. His exact date of birth is not clear, but most likely, it was November 20, 1750. He was the fifth child and the son of Haider Ali from his second wife, Fatima, alias Fakhr-u-Nisa. He was known as the Tiger of Mysore. The story goes that one day while he was out hunting with a French friend, a tiger attacked them. Tipu's gun failed to fire. His dagger also fell down when the tiger jumped upon him. Undaunted, Tipu picked up his dagger and killed the tiger—hence the name the Tiger of Mysore. He also came to be variously known as Sultan Fateh Ali Khan Saheb, Tipu Saheb, Bahadur Khan Tipu Sultan, Fateh Ali Khan, and Tipu Sultan Bahadur. He came to power in 1782, after the death of Haider Ali on December 7, 1782. He became the ruler of Mysore on Sunday, December 22, 1782, in a simple coronation ceremony. He had four wives, from whom he had 16 sons and 8 daughters.

Tipu has been described by Alexander Bateson, historian, thus: "His stature was about five feet eight inches; he had a short neck, square shoulders, and was rather corpulent. His limbs were small, particularly his feet and hands; he had large full eyes, small arched eyebrows, and an aquiline nose; his complexion was fair; and the general expression of his countenance, not void of dignity."

Tipu was a scholar, soldier, poet and a devout Muslim. But his subjects were Hindus. Tipu even built a church for his French allies. Tipu laid the foundation for a dam across the river

Kaveri, where the Krishna Raj Sagar dam stands now. He built roads, public buildings and ports along the coast of Kerala. His domain stretched throughout north Bangalore, including the Nandi Hills, Kanivenarayanpura and Chickballapur. His trade extended to Sri Lanka, Oman, Afghanistan, France, Turkey and Iran. He managed to subdue all the petty kingdoms in the south, defeat the Marathas and the Nizams and was one of the few Indian rulers to ever defeat the British armies. He introduced a new system of weights and measures based on the one introduced by French technicians. He was proficient in many languages, being fluent in Urdu, Kannad, Persian and Arabic. He promoted Persian and Urdu in south India. He modernised his navy and commissioned 20 battleships with 72 cannons each and 20 frigates with 62 guns each. By 1789, most of his ships had copper bottoms, which prolonged the life of the ships considerably. He sent ambassadors to the Ottoman Empire and to France. His treatment of conquered subjects was rather controversial. Haider Ali and Tipu Sultan were known to have ransacked and destroyed Tanjore so badly that it took decades for it to recover.

Tipu Sultan, who had taken over after the death of his father Haider Ali, breached the treaty of Mangalore by not releasing British prisoners, whom he kept chained in what are nowadays known as Colonel Bailey's Dungeons. Some chains and hooks can still be seen attached to the walls to which the British prisoners were kept chained. Tipu planned to attack Nadumkotta, a fortified line of defence built by Dharma Raja of Travancore. The British considered this a declaration of war.

On December 29, 1789, Tipu, with 14,000 troops, attacked the Nadumkotta. In the beginning, he was defeated. While the Mysorian troops were regrouping, the governor, Holland, instead of taking advantage of his victory and mobilising his army, started negotiating with Tipu. General Medows, his replacement, arrived and forcibly removing General Holland. He started mobilising troops at Trichinopoly and planning retaliation against Tipu.

Medows moved from Trichinopoly in late May, when the rains had already started. Tipu had already moved to the higher grounds of Mysore. He managed to capture Coimbatore on the 21st of May without a fight.

On September 2, Tipu left Seringapatam with 40,000 troops. He captured Sathyamanglam and started harassing the British supply and communication lines. At Kaveripattinam, being held by Colonel Maxwell, he could not breach the strong fortification and moved on to rampage in Carnatic. He was chased by Colonel Maxwell and Colonel Medows and landed up at Pondicherry. Here, he tried to garner support from the French, but they were busy with the revolution going on in their own country and paid no heed to him. Meanwhile, Medows reached Madras and gave over his command to Lord Cornwallis.

During the summer of 1790, a Maratha army under Purseram Bhow, along with a detachment of the British from Bombay, took many outposts of Mysore, including Darwar, in September. In early May, they reached the river Tungbhadra. Hari Pant led a second army of 25,000 cavalry and 5,000 infantry, along with a detachment from Madras, in January 1791 from Pune. He joined Cornwallis, who had captured Bangalore and was moving towards Seringapatam.

The Nizam's army, under Mahabat Jung, besieged Koppal in October 1790 but failed as their cannons and gunpowder were very inferior in quality.

The British took control of the Malabar Coast in late 1790. Cornwallis took over the main British army on the 29th of January 1791 at Vellore. He pretended to be going west, and then after deceiving Tipu into thinking he was approaching Bangalore from one side and making him rush back from Pondicherry, he finally approached Bangalore from a totally undefended side. He reached it by the 5th of March and laid siege to it. After three weeks of siege and beating off many attacks from Tipu, he finally took it.

Cornwallis now turned north to meet his ally, the Nizam, to replenish his supplies. On his way back, he noticed that the

Nizam's men were only interested in plundering and not in scouting or helping the British.

The British secured most of the area in and around Bangalore and then moved towards Seringapatam. On the 15th of May, Tipu attacked Cornwallis as he was trying to cross the river Cauvery near Arakere. Cornwallis defeated him, and he was forced to retreat to Seringapatam. By now, Cornwallis's army was near starvation. Seeing no chance of reinforcement from either the Marathas or anywhere else, Cornwallis had to retreat. He did not know that Tipu had successfully prevented communication from the Marathas reaching him. The Marathas reached there just three days later.

On the 11th of June, 2,000 Mysorian troops laid siege to Coimbatore. Lieutenant Chalmers, with just 300 men and inferior gunpowder, fought it out and, with reinforcement from Palgaucherry, took the defenders' supply train. Six thousand more Mysorians arrived, but he held out till the 6th of November. He surrendered after being promised safe conduct, but he and his men were made prisoners when they came out.

Cornwallis had a difficult time with his allies. The Marathas only wanted to pillage and rob and get back the territories they had lost to Tipu's father, Haider Ali. The forces of the Nizam of Hyderabad, according to one British observer, were a "disorderly rabble", more of a hindrance than help and most undisciplined.

On the 25th of January, Cornwallis moved from Savendroog towards Seringapatam. When his massive army reached the plains around Seringapatam, Tipu started firing a barrage of rockets at them. Cornwallis retaliated at night, and Tipu was forced to retreat into the city. Cornwallis laid siege to Seringapatam. He was reinforced by Abercrombie, with an army from Bombay, on February 12. By February 23, Tipu started sending out feelers for peace. On the 24th, he signed the preliminary treaty and the fighting stopped.

According to the terms of the treaty, Tipu was forced to give Cornwallis two of his sons as hostages. On February 26, amongst much fanfare, two of them were handed over. Cornwallis also negotiated the division of Mysore by distributing half of it between the Marathas, the Nizam and the British. Besides losing most of his costal areas, Tipu also had to pay war indemnity. On the 18th of March, Tipu signed the Treaty of Seringapatam, thus ending the Third Anglo-Mysore War.

Tipu Sultan was not a very tolerant or lenient man. He engaged in expansionist attacks against his neighbours and harshly put down any rebellions within his own territory. He was known to have deported whole populations into confinement in Seringapatam. But, maybe, this harshness in his character was a sign of the times. In those days, leniency was easily mistaken for weakness, and no ruler could really afford to appear weak; otherwise, all the enemies would be upon the ruler like vultures. Mainly, he has been described by the British in harsh terms, but there is a doubt about the truth of this as in those times, tolerance was considered synonymous with weakness.

The Fourth Anglo-Mysore War

The fourth, and last, war of Mysore was fought in 1799. The alliance of Tipu Sultan with the French was perceived as a threat by the British. Tipu's troops were outnumbered 4:1 in this war. Tipu had 35,000 soldiers, while the British alone had 60,000 troops. Besides these, they were joined by the troops of the Nizam of Hyderabad and the Marathas. While the British were attacking Seringapatam, the nawab of Hyderabad and the Marathas invaded from the north. One of the divisional commanders of the British army was Colonel Arthur Wellesley, the future duke of Wellington. The British marched into Mysore in 1799 and besieged Seringapatam. On the 8th of March, after they had held off Tipu's advance in the Battle of Seedaseer, they advanced towards Seringapatam. Tipu had already gathered 21,839 soldiers inside the fort and had placed 287 guns on the fortification on the outer walls of the fort. On the 9th of April, General Harris attacked Seringapatam. By the evening of the 24th of April, all the guns on the western wall had been silenced. The British kept up the firing so that the breaches made by their guns could not be repaired.

On the 20th of April, the British East India Company attacked 1,800 Mysore soldiers posted on the banks of the river

Cauvery. Tipu sent a force of 6,000, under a French officer, and they attacked the force of General Harris on April 22. Another force, under Mir Muhammad Hussain and Muhammad Halim, attacked the force of Stuart. The battle lasted several hours. Tipu lost 700 soldiers in this attack, and his infantry retreated. On April 26, supported by artillery fire, the Company's infantry advanced and drove 1,500 Mysorian troops from the west bank of the river. Tipu had lost the infantry battle, and the much-awaited monsoon had not yet arrived.

On the 30th of April, a young lieutenant of the Company troops managed to sneak into Tipu's lines and study the plans of fortification. On the 1st of May, the third phase of the battle started. On the 3rd of May, a breach was reported. Assault began at dawn, and a column of 2,494 Europeans and 1,882 sepoys, led by Lieutenant Lawrence of 77th Regiment, went in. Behind them, Colonel Wellesley was waiting with a reserve party to exploit the gap in the enemy's defence once the storming parties had entered. On the 4th of May, they broke through Tipu's defences. Before this, on the 2nd of May, the British made a concentrated attack on Seringapatam. One of their salvos landed on a magazine of rockets, which exploded and sent up a towering cloud of smoke with cascades of exploding white light. On the 4th of May, Baird led the final attack. He was met by a furious fire of muskets and rockets, but he prevailed. The last charge was made at 12 p.m., under intense fire from Tipu's troops. At this moment, the Company troops hesitated, but General Baird deliberately exposed himself and urged his men to follow him and go forward.

By 1.30, the riverbed had been secured. Tipu's commander Sayyad Gafur was killed and was replaced by Muhammad Kasim.

Tipu was at lunch when he heard that the firangis had progressed from the ramparts to the fortress itself. He rushed to fill and defend the breach and rally his men. He fought valiantly, but his Mysorian troops melted away. They tried to retreat into the inner fort. In the confusion, Tipu was wounded. A British soldier attacked him and managed to wound him, but

Tipu knocked him down by attacking his knee. But the soldier managed to fire his musket, hitting Tipu in the temple and killing him.

Most of the state of Mysore was annexed by the British, the nawab of Hyderabad and the Marathas. The remaining core territory around Mysore and Seringapatam was restored to the Wodeyar dynasty, the rulers of Mysore before Haider Ali became the de facto ruler.

Tipu Sultan was one of the most charismatic rulers of India. There were many factors that led to his defeat. First and foremost, he shifted his style of fighting from mobile aggression to static warfare. His father, Haider Ali, had specialised in guerrilla warfare, and it had created havoc in the British ranks.

Tipu was at a disadvantage in this kind of static warfare as the British had heavier guns, suited more for sieges. They also practiced scientific techniques while conducting sieges, and their engineers and sappers gave them further advantage.

Tipu also failed diplomatically. He could not ally himself with either the Nizam of Hyderabad or the Marathas. He had sent emissaries to the Ottoman Empire, but he failed to provoke Zaman Shah, the ruler of the Ottoman Empire, to go against the British. In fact, the presence of Tipu's agents in Hyderabad, Pune, Persia and Constantinople so spooked the British that they felt he had become a threat to their power in India and decided to finish him off. Even his best allies, the French, let him down as they were more involved with the turmoil going on in their own country and had no time for him.

Today, only the ruins of the fort of Seringapatam remain. The place where Tipu fell is marked by a small marble plaque, put up ironically by the British. There is a small museum looked after by the government inside what at one time was the summer palace of Tipu. The Gumbad marks the place where Haider Ali, Tipu Sultan and all of his family are buried. It is located amidst typical Mughal gardens of that time. There are the dungeons of Colonel Bailey, where Tipu Sultan kept his British prisoners chained to the walls. The story goes that from these dungeons, underground tunnels led to all the places of importance to the ruler, like his summer palace, Sri Ranganath temple, his palace Lal Mahal, etc. These tunnels have been blocked now. There is also the obelisk, which in the former days marked the beginning of the town.

The first rockets were developed by Haider Ali. During the Battle of Pollilur, he used iron tubes for holding the propellant, thus enabling a higher thrust and a longer range, as much as up to two kilometres. Tipu also used them. The British captured them from him and inspired by them, developed the Congreve rocket, which they put to good use in the Napoleonic War.

After the collapse of Mysore, the British became supreme in the south. The fall of Seringapatam also heralded the beginning of the end of the Maratha Confederacy. They had made the biggest mistake of not helping Tipu and, instead, helping the British, who in the end eliminated them also.

References

1. Dromo (n.d.). *Hyder Ali Biography*. Retrieved from http://www.dromo.info/hyderalibio.htm
2. Roy, K. (2004). *India's Historic Battles: From Alexander the Great to Kargil*. Delhi: Permanent Black.
3. Wikipedia (n.d.). *Anglo-Mysore Wars*. Retrieved from http://en.wikipedia.org/wiki/Anglo-Mysore
4. Wikipedia (n.d.). *First Anglo-Mysore War*. Retrieved from http://en.wikipedia.org/wiki/First_Anglo-Mysore_War
5. Wikipedia (n.d.). *Fourth Anglo-Mysore War*. Retrieved from http://en.wikipedia.org/wiki/Fourth_Anglo-Mysore_War
6. Wikipedia (n.d.). *Hyder Ali*. Retrieved from http://en.wikipedia.org/wiki/Hyder_Ali
7. Wikipedia (n.d.). *Second Anglo-Mysore War*. Retrieved from http://en.wikipedia.org/wiki/Second_Anglo-Mysore_War
8. Wikipedia (n.d.). *Third Anglo-Mysore War*. Retrieved from http://en.wikipedia.org/wiki/Third_Anglo-Mysore_War
9. Wikipedia (n.d.). *Tipu Sultan*. Retrieved from http://en.wikipedia.org/wiki/Tipu_Sultan

17 CHAPTER The First Anglo-Sikh War

The First Anglo-Sikh War, fought between 1845 and 1846, resulted in the subjugation of the Sikh kingdom of Maharaja Ranjit Singh. This was one of the last remaining large independent kingdoms in India. The war was fought between the East India Company and the states of Patiala and Jind, or the Sikh Empire.

During the early 19th century, the Sikh kingdom had expanded and had been consolidated by Maharaja Ranjit Singh. He did not trust the British completely, and in a show of wary friendship, he conceded some territory south of the Sutlej. He also built up a strong force to deter invasion from both the British and the Afghans who occupied his other border on the north. He had European mercenary soldiers to train his artillery forces. Being a broadminded and tolerant ruler, he had both Hindus and Muslims in his army. At one time, Peshawar, Multan and even Jammu and Kashmir came under his rule.

During the First Anglo-Afghan War, the Sikhs helped the British against Shuja Shah Durrani in the takeover of Peshawar.

In 1839, Ranjit Singh died. His eldest legitimate son, Kharak Singh, from Maharani Datar Kaur, was crowned but was very unpopular. He ruled only from June 1839 to September 8, 1839. He was removed and put into prison. They say he was poisoned while in prison. He died on the 5th of November 1840. Kunwar Nau Nihal Singh, the son of Kharak Singh and Maharani Chand Kaur, all of 19 years of age, was now crowned. When returning from his father's funeral, while he was passing under the stone arch of the Hazuri Bagh Gate in Lahore Fort, he was injured by falling masonry while his companion was killed. Vizier Dhian Singh carried him into the fort and would not allow even his mother to enter. By the time she and others entered, Nau Nihal Singh was dead.

Sher Singh, the stepbrother of Kharak Singh from Ranjit Singh's wife Rani Mehtab Kaur, daughter of Maharaja Sansar Chand of Kangra, took over. He was challenged by Maharani Chand Kaur as she said that Nau Nihal's wife was carrying and declared herself regent of the unborn child. But when Nau Nihal's wife gave birth to a dead son, all of Chand Kaur's ambitions were destroyed. Later, she was also murdered.

After the death of Ranjit Singh, the Sikh army expanded rapidly from 29,000 men and 192 guns in 1839 to over 80,000 men in 1845. The Sikhs declared themselves as the embodiment of the Khalsa Panth, or the revival of the Sikh nation. With the revival of Serbatt Khalsa, that is, Sikh as a whole, they took power of both the executive and military side of their empire. The British became alarmed at all these developments. They declared that there was perpetual mutiny and rebellion against the Central Court, where intrigues were rife.

Maharaja Sher Singh lived lavishly but could not pay the Khalsas. So he was also murdered in September 1845 by his own cousin Ajit Singh Sindhanwala, who was an officer of the Khalsas. Maharaja Sher Singh had been the son of a Dogra queen. So the Dogras retaliated. There was complete anarchy. Duleep Singh, the youngest son of Ranjit Singh, was crowned. His mother, Jind Kaur, became regent. Vizier Hira Singh was killed while fleeing with loot from the royal treasury. Jind Kaur brought in her own brother Jawaher Singh as the vizier in December 1844. Jawaher Singh was a wastrel.

Meanwhile, Pashaura Singh Kanver, the second-eldest son of Ranjit Singh from his wife Rani Daya Kaur, returned to court and was well received by the public and the army. Jawaher Singh saw this as a threat to Duleep Singh. He first got Pashaura Singh banished to his estates and later got him murdered. The Khalsa army was very upset and forced Jind Kaur to pass the order to kill him for this, and he was beheaded in September 1845 in the presence of his sister and nephew Duleep Singh.

After this, two Dogras, Lal Singh and Tej Singh, became the vizier and the army commander, respectively. They were both high-caste Dogra Hindus who had converted to Sikhism.

After the death of Ranjit Singh in 1843, an uneasy East India Company established a cantonment at Firozpur. They also annexed Sindh. Punjab became suspicious of their motive. Their new political agent in the frontier district, Major George Broadfoot, emphasised disorder and dissension in Punjab. The British East India Company wanted to control Punjab, the last free large bastion left in northern India, which was immensely wealthy to boot. It boasted of the Koh-i-Noor as one of its treasures. But the British hesitated to attack directly as they just did not have enough manpower, until they were forced to do so.

After accusations and counter-accusations between the Sikh durbar and the East India Company, there was a falling out between them, and diplomatic relations were broken. The British started gathering a big force at Firozpur. They already had a division stationed there. Some of their units from their Bengal army started marching towards Firozpur. These consisted of one British unit to every three or four native units. They mostly had light guns from the elite Bengal Horse Artillery.

Perceiving this as a threat, the Sikh army started crossing the Sutlej on the 11th of December 1845. According to them, they were only moving into territory that belonged to them. The Sikhs had Punjabi, Pakhtoon and Kashmiri units, besides the leading, elite Sikh units. Their artillery consisted of heavy guns and gunners who had been trained by European mercenaries.

The movement by the Sikh army across the river was perceived by the British as hostile in nature, and they declared war.

One army, under Tej Singh, advanced towards Firozpur. But surprisingly, it made no attempt to surround or attack the exposed British division there.

On the 18th of December, another force, under Lal Singh, clashed with the Bengal forces, under Gough and Harding, at Mudki. The British won decisively. The next day, the British saw the large Sikh entrenchment outside Firozpur. Gough wanted to attack immediately, but although Harding had placed himself under Gough here, he used his position as governor of Bengal to overrule Gough and forced him to wait for reinforcement from Firozpur. When it arrived, although it was late in the day, Gough attacked. The Sikh artillery caused havoc, but the British infantry fought fiercely. Lal Singh, surprisingly, kept the irregular cavalry, or *ghodachadas*, who were the elite of the Sikh army, away from the battle.

By nightfall, some of Gough's army had managed to get into the Sikh positions while others had been beaten back. Anticipating defeat, Harding ordered all incriminating papers to be burnt. But to his immense surprise, when morning came, he observed that Lal Singh had made no effort to regroup or consolidate his army. Just then, Tej Singh's army came upon the scene. Gough's troops were exhausted and faced defeat, but inexplicably Tej Singh withdrew. He claimed that the British troops and cavalry who were returning to camp for replenishing their ammunition were moving to outflank his own army.

Operations temporarily halted. The British badly needed rest and reinforcement. The Sikhs, dismayed at their defeat, rallied with fresh units. Jind Kaur called 500 select officers and exhorted them to make greater effort.

A detachment of Sikhs crossed the Sutlej near Aliwal and threatened the supply and communication line of Gough. A division, under Sir Henry Smith, was sent to deal with them. The Sikh cavalry attacked Smith's column continually on his march and captured his baggage train, but Smith got reinforcement and, in the Battle of Aliwal, on the 28th of January 1846, he defeated the Sikhs decisively and managed to destroy the Sikh bridgehead.

After being reinforced by Smith's division on the 10th of February, Gough attacked the main Sikh bridgehead at Sobroan. Tej Singh had deserted the Sikh army earlier on in the battle. The Sikhs resisted bravely, but Gough's men eventually breached their ranks. The bridgehead behind them had already been destroyed by either Tej Singh or the British artillery. The Sikhs were trapped. But they fought to the last man. This defeat broke the Sikh army.

After this defeat, on the 9th of March 1856, the treaty of Lahore was signed between the Sikhs and the British East India Company. The Sikhs had to surrender large tracts of valuable land between the Sutlej and Beas Rivers. These lands were known as the Jallandhar Doab. The Lahore Durbar was also forced to pay a war indemnity, or war damages, to the tune of rupees 15 million. Unable to pay it in full, they gave Kashmir, Hazara and all the forts, territories and rights of interest in the hill countries located between the Beas and the Indus to the East India Company in lieu of the rupees 1 crore war indemnity.

Later on, in a separate treaty, The Treaty of Amritsar, the Raja of Jammu, Gulab Singh, purchased Kashmir from the East India Company for rupees 75 lakh and was granted the title of Maharaja of Jammu and Kashmir. Till today, his descendants enjoy this title.

Duleep Singh remained the ruler of Punjab under the regentship of his mother, Maharani Jindan Kaur. At their request, the British remained there and on the 16th of December 1846, the Treaty of Bharowal was signed, granting Jindan Kaur a pension of rupees 1.5 lakh. She was replaced by a British resident supported by a Council of Regency with agents in other cities and regions. So to all purpose, the East India Company gained the control of the government in Punjab and became the de-facto ruler.

Sikh historians claim that to retain their hold on power and on Duleep Singh, Tej Singh and Lal Singh embarked upon a war with deliberate intent of breaking up the Sikh army. Especially, Lal Singh was in contact with some junior British political officers and was betraying state secrets to them. Things like Lal Singh's and Tej Singh's desertion of their army and their refusal to attack when opportunity offered cannot be explained otherwise.

The Sikh kingdom, which had been one of the few still intact after the collapse of the Mughal Empire and constituted a threat to the British East India Company's control of India, had finally been subjugated after this war. But dissension simmered just below the surface, and this led to the Second Anglo-Sikh

War, just two years later, in 1848-49. This war ended in the subjugation of the entire Punjab, which became the North West Frontier Province under the East India Company.

References

1. Wikipedia (n.d.). *First Anglo-Sikh War*. Retrieved from http://en.wikipedia.org/wiki/First_Anglo-Sikh_War
2. Wikipedia (n.d.). *Nau Hihal Singh*. Retrieved from http://en.wikipedia.org/wiki/Nau_Nihal_Singh
3. Wikipedia (n.d.). *Pashaura Singh*. Retrieved from http://en.wikipedia.org/wiki/Pashaura_Singh
4. Wikipedia (n.d.). *Sher Singh*. Retrieved from http://en.wikipedia.org/wiki/sher_singh

18

CHAPTER

Battle of Chillianwala

The Battle of Chillianwala was fought on the 13th of January 1849 between the Sikhs, under General Sher Singh Atariwala, who belonged to the nobility of Punjab, and the forces of the British East India, under Major General Hugh Gough. The Chillianwala region of Punjab lies now in Pakistan. This was considered one of the bloodiest battles of its time, in which, ironically, both sides claimed victory although there was actually a stalemate. For the first time, the British got checkmated and got a shock. They had expected an easy victory, like the other victories, and got an unpleasant surprise.

Major General Hugh Gough, 1st Viscount Gough, KP (Order of St. Patrick), GCSI (The most Exalted Order of the Star of India—Knight Grand Commander), KCB (The Most Honourable Order of the Bath), PC (Member of the Privy Council), was born on November 3, 1779, at Woodstown House in county Limerick to Lieutenant Colonel George Gough and Letitia Bunbury. He came from an old Anglo-Irish family.

Gough was commissioned in the army in August 1794. He had a distinguished career serving in South Africa, West Indies, the Peninsular War, etc. He took part in the capture of Cape Town in 1796 and the capture of Surinam, the attack on Puerto Rico and the Brigand War in St. Lucia. During the Peninsular War, he took part in the Battle of Talavera, the Battle of Barrosa and the Battle of Vitoria. He was decorated by the king of Spain, Charles III, and made a knight after he got wounded at Nevelle.

Promoted to major general in 1830, he came to India in 1837 and took over the Mysore division of the British army. During the Opium War, he was made commander-in-chief of British forces in China. Mount Gough on Hong Kong Island is named after him.

Made a baronet on December 23, 1842, he took over as commander-in-chief of the British forces in India. In December, he defeated the Marathas at Maharajpur and captured more than 50 guns.

In April of 1748, the city of Multan rebelled under Diwan Mulraj. On September 14, 1748, Sher Singh's army also rebelled. The only thing they both had in common was opposition to British control. Already, Chattar Singh, the governor of Hazara and the father of Sher Singh, was rebelling. But as the British held Attock, on the banks of the Indus River, and the passes over the Morgalla Hills, he was unable to move out to Punjab. Sher Singh moved towards Multan and halted near the Chenab River, fortifying the crossing there and waiting for further development.

The East India Company had announced its intention of deposing the young Maharaj Duleep Singh Jee and annexing Punjab. Multan, which had been besieged before, in the First Anglo-Sikh War, in 1848, and the siege lifted afterwards and the besiegers repelled, was besieged once again. But the British forces, under the commander-in-chief, Sir Hugh Gough, and Governor General Lord Dalhousie, delayed an outright attack until the end of the monsoon. Actually, although Dalhousie outranked Gough, he had placed himself under Gough for this war. This gave the Sikhs, under Sher Singh, time to gather reinforcement. Thus, he managed to establish a strong position. Gough took charge on May 21, and on May 22, he attacked Sher Singh's bridgehead on the left bank of the river Chenab near Ramnagar. He was beaten back by the forces of Sher Singh. This victory emboldened Sher Singh further. On the 1st of December, a division of cavalry under Major General Joseph Thankswell crossed over from above Ramnagar. Sher Singh moved against him, and an artillery battle ensued for a whole day between the two forces at Sadullapur. The Sikhs had already left Ramnagar; so Gough's bombardment of Ramnagar was wasted. Gough again compounded the mistake by not attacking the same day but postponing a full-fledged attack for the next day, thus giving the Sikh's a chance to withdraw in the night to the north. Gough now decided to wait for further orders from Dalhousie. Early in January 1849, the British recaptured Multan, although the citadel still held on under Mulraj. In Attock, the Muslim garrison had defected to Amir Dost Mohammad Khan of Afghanistan, who was a supporter of Chattar Singh. With Attock now his ally, Chattar Singh was free to move out of Hazara and towards the south. Gough was ordered by Dalhousie to find and destroy Sher Singh and his forces before they could join up with Chattar Singh's forces. He was told not to wait for reenforcement from Multan, where the citadel was still holding out.

On January 13, hunting for the Sikhs at Rasul, their last reported position, which lies about 137 kilometres northwest of Lahore, on the left bank of the river Jhelum, the Britishers, at about noon, overran a Sikh outpost at a village called Chillianwala. They drove the Sikhs out. But by now, Sher Singh had advanced so far that his forces threatened the flanks of the British, thus forcing them to make a frontal attack.

According to Fredrick Mackenson, the political officer attached to Gough's forces, Sher Singh's army was 23,000 strong, with a contingent of 5,000 irregular cavalry included. Sher Singh also had about 60 guns. But there seems to be a controversy about this number. After the First Anglo-Sikh War, in 1848, the Sikh army had been reduced to 12,000 men and a total of 60 guns. So, according to Sikh historians, Sher Singh's army numbered just 10,000 men.

Sher Singh had deployed one cavalry regiment, nine infantry battalions, some irregular troops and just 20 guns under himself on some low hills and ridges. Two cavalry regiments, 10 infantry battalions and 17 guns under Lal Singh were deployed in the centre. The guns were under camouflage and hidden behind low bushes, scrubs and jungle. On the right stood a brigade from Bannu, one cavalry regiment and four infantry battalions with

11 guns located in two villages. Some irregulars extended the left flank of Sher Singh.

Gough wanted to attack the next day, but even as his men were pitching their camp, the bombardment from the hidden Sikh artillery forced them to attack.

Gough had two infantry divisions with two brigades. Each brigade consisted of one British battalion and two Bengal Native Infantry battalions. Gough also had 66 guns from the Bengal artillery and some Bengal mounted artillery.

On his left, Gough deployed three divisions, with two field artillery batteries and three mounted artillery troops, under Sir Collin Campbell. On the right, he deployed the second division, with a field artillery battery and three horse artillery troops, and some troops under Major General Sir Walter Gilbert. On each flank was a brigade of cavalry, under Major General Joseph Thackwell. The left brigade was commanded by Brigadier White, and the right one commanded by Brigadier Pope, who was old and almost an invalid. In the centre, Gough had two heavy artillery batteries, with eight 18-pounder guns and four 8-inch howitzers. He held in reserve a brigade of Bengal native troops under Brigadier Penney.

The battle began after midday, when the British started advancing at about 3 p.m. Right from the beginning, the brigade on the right was in trouble. Campbell was trying to coordinate his two brigades, but because of the hostile terrain, consisting of forest and scrub land, it was difficult. He took over personally from Brigadier Hoggan, who was commanding on the left, and asked the right-hand brigade to attack with bayonets. Pennycuick's British regiment, 24th Foot, was new to India. It went so fast that it lost contact with the rest of the Brigade and lost its cohesion in the scrub land. They tried to attack head on, but against the desperate Sikh resistance, they had to retreat. They lost the Queen's colours, which were never recovered by either side. Pennycuick's brigade retreated, completely disorganised and demoralised, and Pennycuick himself was killed during the retreat.

The brigade on the left, under Brigadier Hoggan and Campbell himself, fared better. It had 61st Foot and captured several guns and even an elephant. Brigadier White's cavalry made an effective charge. Hoggan's troops finally met up with the troops of the left-hand brigade of Gilbert's division, commanded by Brigadier Mountain, behind the Sikh's centre position.

Gough's right had met with disaster, but Gilbert's men had captured or destroyed several guns. On the right flank, Brigadier Pope had ordered a cavalry charge through the scrub land and forests. This led to utter confusion in his brigade. Panicking, Pope ordered retreat. The British cavalry regiment, 14th Light Dragoons, was routed. The Sikhs chased them and captured four guns. Then they attacked Gilbert's right-hand infantry brigade under Brigadier Godby, from the rear, forcing him to withdraw until the brigade in reserve came to his rescue.

By now, darkness was falling. The Sikhs had been forced to abandon many of their positions, but they were still fighting fiercely. Some of Gough's formation had become ineffective while others were fighting to get out of the noose the Sikhs had thrown around them. Gough had to order a withdrawal. Many of the wounded had to be left behind in the scrubs and the jungle. They were later killed by the Sikh irregulars. The Sikhs also managed to recapture 12 of the guns they had lost earlier in the day.

On that day, the British casualties amounted to 757 killed, 1,651 wounded and 104 missing. The casualties were mostly British, numbering about 1,000 out of the total 2,512. Out of the total, 590 casualties—over 50%—were from 24th Foot.

Among the Sikhs, there were 3,600 dead or wounded in all.

An obelisk at Chillianwala made by the British is dedicated to all those who fell there and has their names upon it.

The result of this battle was that although it was a stalemate, both sides claimed victory.

The Sikhs claimed that they had forced the British to retreat, but in actuality, the British had retreated only after three days and that because of the monsoon.

The Sikhs were the first to disengage. So the British claimed victory.

The British were repulsed on the left and lost several guns. 24th Foot lost its colours, and 14th Light Dragoon was routed.

A British observer on the spot had this to say about the battle: "The Sikhs fought like devils, fierce and untamed.... Such a mass of men I never set eyes on and as plucky as lions: they ran right on the bayonets and stuck their assailants when they were transfixed."

Historian A.H. Amin says, "At Chillianwala a British Army which had a high European troop component, large Sepoy (regiments), sufficient artillery, two heavy cavalry Brigades to ensure that no one could surprise the British Army, excellent logistics, little campaign exhaustion having fought no major battle since assumption of hostilities...failed to defeat the Sikhs.

The Battle of Chillianwala, fought on the 13th of January 1849 is, however, an odd exception and stands out as a battle in which the British failed to defeat their opponents despite having the advantage of numbers, ideal weather and terrain, superior logistics, etc."

The results of this battle were that Gough was blamed totally for everything. He was accused of mishandling the entire situation and was relieved of his command.

The stalemate in this battle and the loss of face suffered by the British inspired and contributed a lot towards the morale of the fighters in the rebellion of 1857, although in this, the Sikhs helped the British to put down the rebellion. The people of India realised that the British were not invincible. They could be defeated if the people were determined to do so.

The people in Britain were so perturbed over this that when, after the famous Charge of the Light Brigade, Lord Lucan remarked, "This is a most serious matter," General Airay is said to have replied, "These sort of things will happen in war. It is nothing to Chillianwala."

Gough personally came in for a lot of criticism after this battle, but when he went back to England, he became a viscount and was granted a pension of 2,000 pounds per annum from the crown and an equal amount from the East India Company.

Later in life, he was made a knight of St. Patrick, was sworn a privy councillor, and was named Knight Grand Commander. In November 1862, he was made field marshal.

References

1. Information retrieved from http://sikhyouth.com/history/anglo-sikh-wars/battle_of_chillianwala (site under construction).
2. Wikipedia (n.d.). *Battle of Chillianwala*. Retrieved from http://en.wikipedia.org/wiki/Battle of Chillianwala
3. Wikipedia (n.d.). *Hugh Gough, 1st Viscount Gough*. Retrieved from http://en.wikipedia.org/wiki/Hugh_Gough,_1st_Viscount_Gough
4. Wikipedia (n.d.). *Lal Singh*. Retrieved from http://en.wikipedia.org/wiki/Lal_Singh

19
CHAPTER
The War of 1857

The War of 1857 was labelled by the Indians as the First War of Independence and called by the British as the Sepoy Mutiny and the Great Rebellion. It was fought between the British East India Company and various northern and central kingdoms of India. Bengal, Bombay Presidency and Madras Presidency remained mainly calm. The Sikhs helped the British. Hyderabad, Mysore, Travancore, Kashmir and Rajputana did not join in. Some of the most famous names belonged to the Rani of Awadh and the Maratha queen of Jhansi. So much so that these ladies became folk heroes in the nationalist movement that followed nearly a century later. It was only after this revolt/war that the British Crown took over from the East India Company and the British Raj truly began.

There were many faces of this war that became household names after this. Tales of bravery, courage and patriotism abounded. Each of these famous names had a reason to join this war.

What exactly were the reasons that led up to this war? One major factor was the Doctrine of Lapse. Under this, the British annexed any state or kingdom if there was no natural, legal heir. Formulated by Lord Dalhousie, it was based on another case, in which the British had annexed the small kingdom of Kittur, in the south, in 1824, when there had been no natural heir and the king had adopted a son. From 1848 to 1856, the British used this act to annex many kingdoms. They annexed Satara in 1848, Sambalpur in 1849, Nagpur and Jhansi in 1854, Tanjore and

Arcot in 1855 and Udaipur in 1856. They also annexed Awadh in 1856 under the pretext that it was not being governed properly.

The old aristocracy suddenly found itself powerless and unemployed. They were forced to become the dependents of the British. Many of them were humiliated and even had their jewels auctioned, like the royal family of Nagpur. So much so that in 1856, Lord Canning announced that the successors of Bahadur Shah Zafar would not be allowed to use the title of king.

Again, the soldiers of the East India Company were also disgruntled. Many of them feared forceful conversion to Christianity. Abolition of sati and encouragement of remarriage of widows were seen as interference in religion. There was also a discrepancy in the pay and perks of the various forces. Men from the Bengal forces were exempt from overseas duties. Also, those soldiers who saw overseas duties in places like Burma (modern-day Myanmar) during the Anglo-Burma War of 1856 were given no foreign-service remuneration, which had been the case so far. In addition, the tradition of a son following his father automatically into the armed forces was stopped. Men were recruited on merit. Promotions for the lower ranks became slower as more and more Europeans joined the ranks of junior officers. Again, a General Service Act now denied them their right to a pension. Although this was meant only for the new recruits, the older ones were suspicious of this. Again, the Bengal army, which consisted mainly of soldiers from the higher castes, was exempt from overseas service and would only serve as far as they could march. The soldiers from Bombay and Madras were not exempt from this.

Another, in fact the most quoted, factor was the new ammunition for the new Enfield rifle, introduced in 1853. Rumours abounded that grease of pork and cows had been used in these. As they had to be opened by biting into them, this would lead to loss of caste and religious ostracism.

The first story of this war is that of Mangal Pandey. Mangal Pandey was a high-class Brahmin soldier born on the 19th of July 1827 in the village of Nagwa in Ballia district, in Uttar Pradesh, in a Bhumihar Brahmin family. At 22 years of age, in 1849, he joined the 6th Corps of the Company's 34th Bengal Native Infantry, as a sepoy. One day, when he refused to allow a low-caste sweeper to drink out of his *lota*, he was taunted by the man that he would lose his caste and become an untouchable like him when he bit into the new bullets being provided by the white sahebs. This led to a strike in Barrackpore in the afternoon, where the soldiers refused to bite the bullet. When Lieutenant Henry Bough, the adjutant, came out to investigate, Mangal Pandey opened fire, but he only managed to kill the horse. Lieutenant Bough also fired from his pistol but also missed. Mangal Pandey drew his talwar (Indian sword) and attacked him. Another two officers who came up were also knocked down. A sepoy, Shaikh Paltu, intervened and tried to stop Pandey and defend the English officer while the other sepoys either just stood around or abused Shaikh Paltu and threw stones and shoes at him. By now, the soldiers from the Quarter Guard had come up and instead of helping the British officers joined in beating them. The commanding officer, General Hearsey come up with his two officer sons and, immediately taking cognisance of what was happening, drew his pistol and threatened to shoot anyone if they did not capture Mangal Pandey. The sepoys obeyed him. Mangal Pandey, fighting for some time, tried to take his own life by putting the muzzle of his musket to his chest and firing with his foot. But he only got injured and his jacket caught fire. He survived, although he was wounded. He was arrested and held by Sheikh Paltu, the only Indian who refused to join the strike. The other soldiers who had been asked to arrest Mangal Pandey refused to do so. Mangal Pandey and his friends were court-martialled on 6th of April and were to be hanged on the 18th, but they were hanged fully 10 days ahead of time, on the 8th, as the British feared an uprising and protest. The regiment was stripped of its uniform and disbanded.

The sepoys with Mangal Pandey had many grievances. They were dissatisfied with the pay and perquisites they were getting. They were scared of forcible conversion to Christianity as General Wheeler of 34th British Native Infantry, a zealous Christian, had distributed Bibles in Urdu and Devnagari. And of course, they were suspicious of the new cartridges, which were supposed to be greased with animal fat.

Meerut was the biggest cantonment of the British. It had 2,357 Indian sepoys and 2,038 British soldiers and 12 British-manned guns. On 24th of April, Lieutenant Colonel George Carmichael Smyth ordered 90 of his men to parade and drill and use the disputed cartridges. All except five refused. On May 9, the remaining 85 were court-martialled and given 10 years of hard labour. The entire garrison watched as they were stripped of their uniforms and put in shackles.

The next day was a Sunday. Some of the soldiers warned the British, but they ignored the warning and no action was taken. There was unrest in the bazaars. Some prostitutes taunted the soldiers. A building was set on fire. In the evening, when the British were preparing for the church or for recreation, 3rd Cavalry broke into revolt. They killed their European officers and then attacked the civilian quarters of the Europeans. Four civilians, eight women and four children, were killed. Some Indian civilians trying to defend their masters died.

The soldiers spread out into the bazaar. The kotwal, Dhan Singh Gujar, opened the gates of the city jail. A total of 50 European men, women and children were killed. The sepoys released their 85 comrades and 800 other criminals. Some trusted sepoys of 11th Bengal Native Infantry escorted some of the British officers, women and children to safety before joining in the rebellion. Some of the British families escaped to Rampur and took refuge with the nawab. The rebels marched off to Delhi to proclaim Bahadur Shah Zafar, the last Mughal, as emperor. No effort was made to pursue them.

On May 11, the revolt spread to Delhi. Three battalions of Native Infantry joined the rebels. Others just stood by doing nothing. They did not actively join the rebels, but they also did not obey the British.

Nine British officers were in-charge of the arsenal, or ammunition dump, in Delhi. Fearing that it might fall into the hands of the rebels, these officers blew it up. The rebels managed to get only a little of the ammunition and one magazine, which was located three kilometres out of Delhi. They managed to lay their hands on 3,000 barrels of gunpowder also.

The British retreated to Karnal. On the way, some villagers helped them while others robbed and murdered them.

The next day, the rebels proclaimed Bahadur Shah Zafar as the king. Bahadur Shah's servants found around 50 Europeans hiding and killed them under a Peepal tree in his courtyard.

The revolt spread fast to Agra, Benaras and Allahabad. Ambala went up in flames. There was utter chaos. The Awadhis wanted to retain their power.

The British were supported by Aga Khan, the Sikhs and the Pathans from the North West Frontier Province. They helped them to recapture Delhi. The Sikhs helped the British because they wanted revenge upon the Purabias (Easterners), who had beaten them with British help eight years before. They did not want the reinstatement of Mughal rule. After all, they had originally come about as an answer against Mughal rule.

At that time, the face of Delhi was Bahadur Shah Zafar, the last Mughal ruler. Born in Delhi on October 14, 1775, he was the son of Akbar Shah II and a Rajput lady, Lal Bai. At the time of the uprising, he was 82 years old, but he became the symbol of the revolt around which the others gathered. According to William Dalrymple, 300 sepoys from Meerut rode into Delhi, massacred men women and children and proclaimed Bahadur Shah Zafar emperor. He was the rallying point for both the Muslims and the Hindus.

From July 1 to September 21, the Company forces in Delhi were under siege. On August 16, Sikh and Pakhtoon soldiers under John Nocholson reinforced the besieged forces on the ridge. On August 30, the British offered peace terms to the rebels, which were rejected. On September 14, the British soldiers entered Delhi through Kashmere Gate. There was heavy street fighting. Bahadur Shah Zafar fled to Humayun's Tomb. The next day, William Hodson shot his two sons Mirza Mughal and Mirza Khazir Sultan and his grandson Mirza Abu Bakar at Khooni Darwaza.

The third famous face of the 1857 War of Independence is that of Rani Laxmi Bai of Jhansi. She was born into a Maharashtrian Brahmin family on probably the 19th of November 1828 in Benaras/Varanasi. Her father was Moropant Tambe and her mother was Bhagirathi Bai. She was christened Manikarnika. Bhagarathi Bai died when Manikarnika was just four. Her father, Moropant Tambe, worked in the court of the *peshwa* of Bithoor, who brought up Manikarnika along with his own sons and treated her like a daughter. He called her Chhabili because of her quicksilver personality. Manikarnika learnt archery, fencing, riding, self-defence, shooting, etc.

At the age of 14, Manikarnika was married to the 40-year-old Gangadhar Rao, the raja of Jhansi. At the time of her marriage, keeping with tradition, her name was changed to Laxmi Bai. In 1851, she had a son named Damodar Rao, who unfortunately died after four months. Gangadhar Rao was heartbroken and took to his bed. On his deathbed, he adopted Anand Rao the son of his cousin, and changed his name to Damodar. He adopted the child in the presence of the British resident and requested the British to recognise his young queen as the regent and recognise his adopted son as the ruler of Jhansi. By then, Lord Dalhousie had implemented the Doctrine of Lapse and refused to do so. The British annexed the state.

The rani was pensioned off and given an annual allowance of rupees 60,000 and told to leave the palace and the fort in Jhansi.

On the 10th of May, the rebellion started prematurely in Meerut. With British permission, the rani raised a private army for her own protection and that of Jhansi.

At Jhansi, the British took refuge in the Star Fort. They sent a message to the rani to help them and to give them refuge. It is said the messenger was killed and the rebels sent a decoy, who lured the British to Jokan Bagh, where all of them were massacred. Only one Anglo-Indian lady managed to escape, dressed in native dress. The men of 12th Bengal Native Infantry, after this, extorted money from the rani and moved off to join the rebellion. Meanwhile, the British wrote to the rani to manage Jhansi for them until they could take over.

At Cawnpur (Kanpur), General Wheeler, married to an Indian girl, was besieged by Nana Saheb for three weeks. Finally, Nana Saheb offered safe passage to the besieged British. But on June 27, when the men, women and children were in boats on the way to Allahabad, he got them all shot from the banks. In Cawnpur itself, five men and 200 women and children were imprisoned in the Bibighar where, within a week, 25 of them died of Cholera. On the 15th of July, when it became clear that Nana would have to leave Cawnpur, he decided to murder the hostages. The Indian sepoys refused to murder in cold blood; so two Muslim butchers and two Hindu peasants and one of Nana's guards killed all of them and threw their bodies into a well. The rest who were killed on the Ganga were thrown into the river.

In September and October 1857, the rani defended Jhansi successfully against an attack from Datia and Orchha. The rani asked the British for help, but there was no communication from them. Finally, on February 3, Sir Hugh Rose released Saugar. In March 1858, he reached Jhansi and asked the rani to hand it over to him. She refused to do so and declared independence. So on the 23rd of March he laid siege to Jhansi.

Meanwhile, the rani had fortified the defences of Jhansi. She had established many foundries for making cannons and raised an army, which even had contingents of women. The rani sent word to Tantia Tope, who arrived with an army of 20,000 strong and many heavy guns. Unfortunately, his guns got bogged down in sand and he was badly defeated and withdrew. The rani was betrayed by one of her disgruntled gatekeepers, who opened the gates for the British. There was heavy street fighting. The braves of Jhansi fought in every lane, every house and every room. But they were overwhelmed. The rani was forced to leave. She jumped on her horse from the battlement of the fort and with her adopted son, Damodar, tied securely to her back, she fled from Jhansi to Kalpi, where she joined Tantia Tope and Rao Saheb, the nephew of Nana.

On May 22, the British attacked Kalpi. Rao Saheb and others were busy enjoying themselves and celebrating. The rani was the only one ready, and she defended Kalpi bravely but lost against heavy odds. They had to abandon Kalpi, and all of them came to Gwalior. Maharaja Scindhia of Gwalior had already abandoned the place. On the 16th of June 1858, Laxmibai captured the fort of Gwalior from the Scindias, who supported the British. Here, she and her allies proclaimed Nana as *peshwa* and Rao Saheb as his *subedar*, or governor, in Gwalior.

The rani died a martyr's death, while bravely fighting against Sir Hugh Rose, on the 18th of June in the Second Battle of Gwalior. She had her adopted son, Damodar Rao, strapped to her back and wielded a sword in each hand while holding the leather bridle in her mouth. While dying, she handed him over to a trusted lieutenant of hers and requested him to kill her and burn her body so that the British could not defile it. Raghunath Rao wielded the final stroke and then carried her body to the hut of a nearby ascetic, where they burned her before the British could get to her. She was just 23 years of age. Eye witnesses compared her to Joan of Arc.

According to Colonel Mallison, in his *History of Indian Mutiny* (volume 3, 1878), "Whatever her faults in British eyes may have been, her countrymen will ever remember that she was driven by ill-treatment into rebellion, and that she lived and died for her country."

On 1st of July, Indore revolted. Thirty-nine European residents were killed while others escaped. On the 7th of July, 35 British soldiers were killed in Jhelum in Punjab. On the 9th of July, most of a brigade at Sialkot rebelled and moved towards Delhi. Three days later, John Nicholson, with an equal force, killed 1,100 of the men who were trapped on an island in the Battle of Trimmu Ghat.

In Jaunpur, Raghu Raj of Dobhi played a big part. In Bihar, the Lion of Bihar, Babu Kunwar Singh of Jagdishpur, Arrah, played a big role and was the face of the rebellion. Born in November 1777, he was already 82 years old when he joined the rebellion. He was the son of Raja Sahabzada Singh and Rani

Panchratan Devi in Jagdishpur, in Shahabad, now in Bhojpur, Bihar.

On the 25th of July, rebellion broke out in Danapur. Babu Kunwar Singh took over the command of the revolt here on the 5th of July. On the 7th of July, he occupied Arrah. On the 29th of July, 400 men were sent from Danapur to relieve Arrah. On the 30th of July, Major Vincent Eyre reached Buxar. On August 2, he was ambushed. After a hard fight and a charge by 5th Fusiliers, they captured Arrah on August 3. Major Eyre captured and destroyed Jagdishpur also.

Babu Kunwar Singh reached Lucknow in December 1857. He fought and harried the British for a whole year. There is a story about him that while crossing the river Ganga, he was shot in his wrist. He took out his sword and, declaring that the hand was now useless to him and would probably get gangrenous, he chopped off his hand from the elbow and offered it to the river Ganga.

Kunwar Singh was also helped by the Rajputs of Dobhi, where one of his daughters was married. After the war was over, the British called all of them for a conference in a mangrove and played foul by hanging them. Only one man, Maha Singh, who was a giant, managed to escape by elbowing his captors and jumping upon a horse and riding bareback for life. The Rajputs of Dobhi area were forbidden after this from keeping any weapons or knives more than six inches in length.

In March 1858, Kunwar Singh occupied Azamgarh. He had to abandon this soon and was pursued by Brigadier Douglas. Kunwar Singh retreated towards Arrah. On April 23, he had his last victory, over a force led by Captain Le Grand near Jagdishpur. On the 26th of April 1858, he died in his village, some say, of gangrene. His brother Amar Singh carried on his campaign after this.

Begum Hazrat Mahal was the face of Lucknow and Awadh during this war. She was born Muhammadi Khanum in Faizabad, Awadh. A courtesan by profession, she joined the royal harem of Nawab Wajid Ali Shah of Awadh as a *khawasin* when she was sold by her parents to Royal agents. Later, she was promoted to the rank of pari and became a royal concubine. She got the name of Begum Hazrat Mahal when her son Birjis Qudra was born.

When the nawab of Awadh was exiled by the British to Calcutta, Begum Hazrat Mahal divorced him and took over the administration of Awadh herself. In 1857, she took control of Lucknow and declared her son nawab of Awadh.

Lucknow was retaken by the British in March 1858. Begum Hazrat Mahal retreated to Faizabad, where she joined Nana Saheb and the maulvi of Faizabad in the attack on Shahjahanabad. Later on, she was forced to retreat to Nepal with Nana Saheb and Tantia Tope, where she died in 1879 and was buried in the grounds of the Jama Masjid in Kathmandu.

On the 8th of July 1858, a peace treaty was signed and the rebellion ended. The last of the rebels were defeated in Gwalior on the 20th of June.

The British extracted stiff penalties from the defeated Indians and banned the carrying of muskets or any sharp knife longer than six inches. They banned processions, etc., also. In August, by the Government of India Act of 1858, the company was formally dissolved and the ruling power transferred to the Crown. Queen Victoria formally took the title of Empress of India.

References

1. Verma, V. (1993). *Jhansi ki Rani*. New Delhi: Prabhat Prakashan.
2. Wikipedia (n.d.). *Babu Kunwar Singh*. Retrieved from http://en.wikipedia.org/wiki/Babu_Kunwar_Singh
3. Wikipedia (n.d.). *Begum Hazrat Mahal*. Retrieved from http://en.wikipedia.org/wiki/Begum_Hazrat_Mahal
4. Wikipedia (n.d.). *Indian Rebellion of 1857*. Retrieved from http://en.wikipedia.org/wiki/Indian_Rebellion_of_1857
5. Wikipedia (n.d.). *Mangal Pandey*. Retrieved from http://en.wikipedia.org/wiki/Mangal_Pandey
6. Wikipedia (n.d.). *Rani Lakshmibai*. Retrieved from http://en.wikipedia.org/wiki/Rani_Lakshmi_Bai

20

CHAPTER

1948, First Indo-Pak War

This was the first of the four wars fought so far between India and Pakistan. Known as the First Kashmir War also, this was fought in 1947-48. On October 22, 1947, Pakistani forces crossed the border, claiming to ostensibly suppress a rebellion in the southeast of the kingdom. Local tribesmen and the Pakistani forces moved towards Srinagar. On reaching Uri, they encountered our defensive forces.

Raja Hari Singh, the Hindu ruler of a primarily Muslim state of Kashmir, who had so far been sitting on the fence about his decision to join one of the two countries, decided to appeal to India for help and signed the Instrument of Accession. As the British government was still very much evident, they finally stopped the Pakistani forces. A formal ceasefire was declared at 23.59 hours on the night of 1-2 January 1949.

This is all in a nutshell, but let us go into a little more detail.

History

Prior to 1815, J&K consisted of 22 small, independent states, 16 of which were Hindu states while six were Muslim states ruled by Rajput kings. All these states were the vassals of the Mughal Empire since the time of Akbar. For some time, some of them were controlled by the state of Kangra, in Himachal Pradesh. During the reign of Ranjit Singh, for some time, they even came under Sikh rule. After the First Anglo-Sikh War, in 1845-46, the Treaty of Lahore was signed. The Sikhs, who lost, could not pay the indemnity of rupees 1-2 million; so the East India Company allowed the Dogra ruler, Gulab Singh, to buy Kashmir for rupees 750,000. It was his dynasty that ruled here till the partition of India in 1947. It was when the Khyber and Pakhtoon tribals, backed by the regular Pakistani soldiers, invaded that Raja Hari Singh turned to India for help. When the maharaja had appealed to Pakistan to stop the invaders, Pakistan had refused, saying they were tribals and not its regular troops. When the Indians sent in their regular troops to defend Kashmir, the then army chief of Pakistan, General Douglas Gracy, who was a Britisher, refused to send troops ordered by Muhammad Ali Jinnah as he said that the Indian forces occupying Kashmir represented the British Crown. By the time Pakistan got around this, three-fourths of Kashmir was in Indian hands. Only Gilgit and Baltistan were secured by the Gilgit Scouts, belonging to Pakistan.

Initial invasion: It was a very ding-dong battle. State forces in Muzaffarabad and Domel were defeated. The invaders, instead of advancing towards Srinagar, got busy looting and revelling.

After Raja Hari Singh ceded to India, Indians airlifted troops to Srinagar, reinforcing the state force there, which defeated the tribal invaders. They outflanked the invaders with armoured cars and recaptured Baramulla and Uri.

Gilgit Scouts joined the invading forces in Gilgit. They were joined by troops from Chitral. The Mehtar (ruler) of Chitral had acceded to Pakistan.

Mirpur was captured on the 25th of November 1947 by the tribal forces, who then besieged Poonch. This siege of Poonch lasted till the 20th of November 1948.

Tribal troops captured Jhanger and then attacked Naushera and Uri but were unsuccessful. The Indians captured Chhambh. The Indian forces counter-attacked and captured Jhanger and Rajouri under Operation Vijay.

After this, the Gilgit Scouts besieged north Skardu.

In Jhanger, the Indian troops held on against many counter-attacks and even when regular Pakistani troops were used. In the Kashmir Valley, they recaptured Tithwal.

The Gilgit Scouts laid siege to Leh, and they captured Kargil in Operations Gulab and Erazze.

The Indians captured Keran and Gurais in two separate operations.

The besieged troops in Poonch broke out and joined up with the forces outside.

The Kashmir state forces defended Skardu until August, when the Chitral forces, under Mata-ul-Mulk, with the help of artillery captured it. This operation was first called Operation Duck; and then, at the behest of General Cariappa, the name was changed to Operation Bison.

In Ladhak, 77 Parachute Brigade, under Brigadier Atal, Maha Vir Chakra (MVC), tried to capture Zoji La (in Ladhaki, *la* means pass).

General Timmayya daringly moved M5 Stuart Light Tanks of the 7th Cavalry in a dismantled condition through Srinagar to Zoji La. To maintain secrecy, when the tanks were being moved through Srinagar, a curfew was declared and they were moved in the dead of the night. On the 1st of November, they made a surprise attack. Tanks have never been used at such heights. Two regiments of 25 pounders and a regiment of 3.7-inch guns forced the Pakistani forces to back off to Matyan and Dras. On the 24th of November, these tank groups linked up with Indian troops from Leh.

Poonch was finally relieved after a siege of one year. Dras was captured, and on the 31st of December 1948, a ceasefire was declared. Nehru asked the United Nations to intervene. Fifteen hundred soldiers from both sides died in this battle.

There were many heroes in the war in various sectors. Here are some lines about them.

Major Somnath Sharma, PVC

The hero of Srinagar, Major Somnath Sharma was awarded the Param Vir Chakra (PVC) posthumously. Born in 1923, he came from a distinguished family of army men. His father was Major General Amarnath Sharma, who retired as director of medical services of the army. One of his brothers, General Vishwanath

Sharma, was chief of army staff from 1988 to 1990. Another of his brothers, Lieutenant General Surindernath Sharma, retired as the engineer-in-chief. Even his sister, Major Kamla Tiwari, served as a doctor in the army. Major Somnath Sharma was commissioned into the 8th Battalion of 19th Hyderabad (which later became 4 Kumaon) on February 22, 1942. Major Somnath Sharma's company was airlifted to Srinagar on the 31st of October 1947. He had suffered an injury to his right hand during a game of hockey, and it was in plaster. When on the 3rd of November, Major Sharma's D company of 4 Kumaon was ordered to Badgam village in Kashmir Valley, a tribal lashkar of 700 raiders surrounded it from the Gulmarg side. Major Sharma knew the importance of holding on. Otherwise, Srinagar and its airport would be lost and reinforcement would not be able to come into the valley.

Outnumbered 7 to 1, Major Somnath Sharma ran from post to post exposing himself and encouraging his men. When casualties became too high, with his right hand still in plaster, he took on the task of filling the magazines for his men. His last message to the brigade headquarters was:

> "The enemy are only 50 yards from us. We are heavily outnumbered. We are under devastating fire. I shall not withdraw an inch but will fight to our last man and our last round."

The next moment, a mortar shell exploded on the ammunition pile near him and killed him.

By the time relief in the form of 1st Battalion of Kashmir Regiment reached the position that had been held by Major Somnath Sharma and his men, it had been overrun, but there had been 200 enemy casualties. The raiders had been halted, and this courageous act bought precious time for the Indian troops to land at Srinagar. Major Sharma prevented the fall of Srinagar and the Kashmir Valley. He was awarded the PVC posthumously.

Lieutenant Ram Ragobha Rane, PVC

The hero of Rajouri sector was Lieutenant R.R. Rane, decorated with the PVC.

Lieutenant R.R. Rane was born on the 26th of June 1918 at Chendia, in Karnataka. He was commissioned on the 15th of December 1947 in the Corps of Engineers. When the attack on Rajouri was made on the 8th of April 1948, Lieutenant Rane discovered that there were too many mines in the way of the advance. On the 10th, he removed a big roadblock by blasting it with dynamite. He had been clearing mines the whole of 8th, right through the night, and then on the 9th for another 12 hours continuously, and then to help facilitate the advance, Lieutenant Rane tied himself below a tank to guide them. On the 11th, he worked 17 hours to open the road to Chingas and beyond. He suffered from permanent hearing loss because of this strategy and was awarded the PVC.

Brigadier Pritam Singh, MC; Air Commodore "Baba" Mehar Singh, MVC; and Air Vice Marshal Subroto Mukherjee

The hero's of Poonch were Brigadier Pritam Singh, Military Cross (MC); Air Commodore "Baba" Mehar Singh, Maha Vir Chakra (MVC); and Air Vice Marshal Subroto Mukherjee, who himself carried out a daring trial landing in a Harvard plane on the makeshift airfield at Poonch. After this, under the aegis of Air Commodore "Baba" Mehar Singh and Brigadier Pritam Singh, Dakotas (DC 3) started landing, first by day and then even by night. The fledgeling Indian Air Force made an air bridge, supplying the beleaguered Poonch garrison not only with supplies but even with complete sections of mountain artillery. They brought in supplies and ferried out refugees. They brought in 25-pounder guns. Poonch was called the "Tobruk" of Kashmir. It never fell.

Air Commodore "Baba" Mehar Singh was a legend in his time. He flew the first Dakota, which landed on the makeshift airstrip at Leh. He also undertook the conversion of Dakotas to bombers. In the Second World War, he had received a Distinguished Service Order (DSO). He was the first recipient of the MVC from the Air Force. He died in a tragic civilian air crash in 1952.

Naik Yadunath Singh, PVC

Another hero of this same Rajouri sector was Naik Yadunath Singh.

The citation for the PVC awarded to him reads:

Naik Jadunath Singh

1st Battalion, Rajput Regiment (No 27373)

At No 2 picquet on Taindhar on 6 February 1948, No 27373 Naik Jadunath Singh was in command of a forward section post, which bore the full brunt of the enemy attack. Nine men against overwhelming odds garrisoned the little post. The enemy launched its attack in successive waves and with great ferocity to overcome this post. The first wave swept up to the post in a furious attack. Displaying great valour and superb qualities of leadership Naik Jadunath Singh so used the small force at his disposal that the enemy retired in utter confusion. Four of his men were wounded but Naik Jadunath Singh again showed his qualities of good leadership by reorganizing the battered force under him, for meeting another onslaught. His coolness and courage were of such an order that the men rallied and were ready for the second attack which came with greater determination and in larger number than the preceding one. Though hopelessly outnumbered, this post under the gallant leadership of Naik Jadunath Singh resisted. All were wounded, and Naik Jadunath Singh, though wounded in the right arm, personally took over the Bren gun from the wounded Bren gunner. The enemy was right on the walls of the post but Naik Jadunath Singh once again showed outstanding ability and valour of the highest order in action. By his complete disregard for his personal safety and example of coolness and courage, he encouraged his men to fight. His fire was so devastating, that what looked like impending defeat was turned into a victory and the enemy retreated in chaos leaving the dead and wounded littered on the ground. With this act of supreme heroism and outstanding example of leadership and determination, Naik Jadunath Singh saved the post from the second assault. By this time, all men in the post were casualties. The enemy put in his third and final attack in undiminished numbers and determination to capture this post.

Naik Jadunath Singh, now wounded, prepared literally single-handed to give battle for the third time. With great courage and determination, he came out of the sangar and finally with the sten-gun, made a most magnificent single-handed charge on the advancing enemy, who, completely taken by surprise, fled in disorder. Naik Jadunath Singh, however, met his gallant death in his third and last charge when two bullets hit him in the head and chest. Thus, charging single-handedly at the advancing enemy, this Non-Commissioned Officer, performed the highest act of gallantry and self-sacrifice and by so doing saved his section—nay, his whole picquet from being overrun by the enemy at the most critical stage in the battle for the defence of Naushera.

Brigadier Mohammad Usman, MVC

Brigadier Mohammad Usman, MVC, was the highest-ranking officer to be killed in this battle. He was known as the Lion of Naushera. He was born on July 15, 1912, at Bibipur, Azamgarh, UP. He was commissioned in Baluch Regiment. At the time of partition, in spite of being given the lure of becoming the Pakistani army chief, he transferred to the Dogras and stayed back in India. At the time of the 1947 war, he was commanding 77 Para Brigade. Later, they gave him 50 Para Brigade.

Brigadier Usman has been hailed all over India as the hero of Naushera. When Jhanger was lost for some time to the enemy, Brigadier Usman swore that he would not sleep on a cot till it was retaken, and he did so. His 50th Brigade had been earmarked for the recapture of Jhanger. The order of the day issued by him just before the assault gives us a picture of the man himself.

"Comrades of 50 Para Brigade.

Time has come when our planning and preparation for the recapture of Jhanger is to be put to test. It is not an easy task but I am confident of success—because our plan is sound and our preparations have been good. More so because I have complete confidence in you all to do your best to recapture the ground we lost on 24th December and to retrieve the honour of our arms.

The hopes and the aspirations of our countrymen are based upon our efforts. We must not falter—we must not fail them.

To every man upon this earth,

Death cometh sooner or late;

And how man can die better

Than facing fearful odds,

For the ashes of his father

And the temples of his Gods.

So forward friends, fearless we go to Jhanger. India expects every one to do his duty.

Jai Hind!

Mohammad Usman

Brigadier"

Usman was a patriotic Indian, and the Pakistanis had labelled him a traitor and put a reward on his head. So much so that they even spread rumours about his death. When a wire was sent to him enquiring about his welfare, he replied, "fit and flourishing—still in the world of the living". Ironically, he died a few hours before this signal was received at Army Headquarters.

Usman was given a full state funeral in Delhi. Posthumously awarded MVC, he is buried in a grave in Jamia Millia Islamic Campus in New Delhi. A film was made on him by Upender Sood. His birth centenary was celebrated by the army at Jhajjar. A Paramotor Expedition was organised by the Gurkha Training Centre to commemorate the day.

Jamadar Nand Singh, VC, MVC

Jamadar Nand Singh holds a unique position in the annals of 1947 war. He was the one man who had won the Victoria Cross in the Second World War and the MVC in this war posthumously. The citation for the Victoria Cross reads:

On 11/12 March 1944 on the Maungdaw-Buthidaung Road, Burma (now Myanmar), Naik Nand Singh, commanding a leading section of the attack, was ordered to recapture a position gained by the enemy. He led his section up a very steep knife-edged ridge under very heavy machine-gun and rifle fire and although wounded in the thigh, captured the first trench. He then crawled forward alone and, wounded again in the face and shoulder, nevertheless captured the second and third trenches.

In the war of 1947, on the 12th of December, Jamadar Nand Singh led his platoon of D Company in a desperate but successful attack to extricate his battalion from an ambush in the hills southeast of Uri. Though his platoon was successful, Nand Singh was mortally wounded and died. The Pakistanis recognized him from the Victoria Cross ribbon he wore. They took his body to Muzaffarabad and paraded it through the town spreadeagled upon a truck, proclaiming through a hailer that this would be the fate of all Victoria Cross holders of India. Then, they threw his body on a garbage heap. Unfortunately, it was never recovered.

Nand Singh belonged to the village Bahadurpur, now in district Mansa in Punjab. A bus stand in the town of Bereta has been named in his memory as "Shaheed Nand Singh Victoria Bus Stand". A statue of his also stands at the chowk known as Fauji Chowk in Bhatinda.

In this war, our fledgling air force played a vital part in giving support to our troops and also in carrying reinforcement to various sectors as also vital supplies and weapons required.

Even the navy played a small part when one of our tanks fell off a raft in a river and two naval divers had to be flown in from Bombay to locate it and recover it.

References

1. Sinha, S.K. (2002). *Operation Rescue—Military Operations in Jammu & Kashmir 1947-49*. New Delhi: Vision Books.
2. Wikipedia (n.d.). *Indo-Pakistani War of 1947*. Retrieved from http://en.wikipedia.org/wiki/Indo-Pakistani_War_of_1947
3. Wikipedia (n.d.). *Jadu Nath Singh*. Retrieved from http://en.wikipedia.org/wiki/Jadu_Nath_Singh
4. Wikipedia (n.d.). *Military Operations in Poonch (1948)*. Retrieved from http://en.wikipedia.org/wiki/Military_operations_in_Poonch_(1948)

5. Wikipedia (n.d.). *Mohammad Usman*. Retrieved from http://en.wikipedia.org/wiki/Mohammad_Usman
6. Wikipedia (n.d.). *Nand Singh*. Retrieved from http://en.wikipedia.org/wiki/Nand_Singh
7. Wikipedia (n.d.). *Rama Raghoba Rane*. Retrieved from http://en.wikipedia.org/wiki/Rama_Raghoba_Rane
8. Wikipedia (n.d.). *Som Nath Sharma*. Retrieved from http://en.wikipedia.org/wiki/Som_Nath_Sharma

21 CHAPTER The Debacle of the Sino-Indian War of 1962

This Sino-Indian war was fought between India and China in 1962. It was fought on two fronts. The disputed region of Aksai-Chin, a piece of territory the size of Switzerland that lies between the Chinese autonomous region of Xinjiang and Tibet (which was taken over by China in the early 1950s) and the North Eastern Frontier Agency (NEFA), the present-day Arunachal Pradesh, which the Chinese overran in 1962.

Aksai-Chin is a desert of salt flats, 5,000 metres above sea level. Arunachal Pradesh has many peaks over 7,000 metres high. Here, the Chinese armies possessed one of the highest ridges.

One of the major causes that led to this war was the dispute over the sovereignty of Aksai-Chin and Arunachal Pradesh. India said Aksai-Chin belonged to Kashmir. The Chinese said it belonged to Xinjiang. In 1958-59, the Chinese built a road connecting Tibet to Xinjiang, which ran right through Aksai-Chin.

The history of this area is rather mixed up. In 1865, during the British rule, W.H. Johnson, a civil servant with the Survey of India, proposed the "Johnson Line". This put Aksai-Chin in Kashmir. In the 19th century, when the Russians and the British were vying for power in Central Asia, the British handed over Aksai-Chin to China. They created a new border called the McCartney-MacDonald Line.

In 1918, after the Bolshevik Revolution in Russia, the British redrew the border as the original Johnson Line, but this was only on paper. The Chinese kept possession of the area. By 1947, Johnson Line had become India's official western boundary.

In 1956-57, China constructed a road through Aksai-Chin connecting Tibet to Xinjiang. The region was easily accessible to the Chinese, but the Indians faced negotiating the Karakoram Range of mountains.

On the eastern front in NEFA in 1918, Henry McMahon drew a line south of the Himalayas, which we traditionally claim as our boundary. A conference was held in 1913 at Shimla, in which China, India and Tibet sat down to talk over the disputed areas. According to the Chinese, these areas, especially Tawang, belonged to Tibet and, in consequence, to China. But it was only in the 1930s that the British officially started showing the McMahon Line as the official boundary on maps of the region. In 1950, the Indian Government started patrolling the area actively.

In 1956, the then Chinese prime minister, Zhou Enlai, stated categorically that he had no claim on Indian-controlled territory. Later on, he said that Aksai-Chin was already under Chinese control.

In 1950, Tibet was annexed, and it was then that Pandit Nehru declared the McMahon Line as the border.

In 1959, the Dalai Lama escaped from Tibet, took refuge in India and settled in Dharamshala, in Himachal Pradesh.

In 1960, China refused to acknowledge the McMahon Line and, in fact, asked India to drop claim to Aksai-Chin and NEFA. According to Colonel Anil Athale, author of the official Indian history of the 1962 Sino-Indian conflict, China even sent large quantities of non-military supplies to Tibet through the port of Calcutta.

Military incidents and skirmishes flared up in summer and autumn of 1962. In May, the Indian Air Force was categorically told not to prepare for close air support, although it was ready for attack. India did not want escalation of war. It wanted to create and garner sympathy in the United States as it had lost this after its operation in Goa in 1961.

By July, orders were passed to fire if attacked or threatened.

In June 1962, Indians established an outpost at Dhola, north of the McMahon Line but south of the ridges, interpreted by them as the border and the McMahon Line.

The Chinese perceived this as aggression into their territory. In August 1962, Brigadier D.K. Palit ruled out war in the near future with China. In September 1962, when ordered to throw out the Chinese from Thang La, Major General Dhillon said, "Experience in Ladakh has shown that a few rounds fired at the Chinese would cause them to run away." So the Indian companies were totally unprepared when the attack on Yamtso La occurred.

On the 8th of October, the Chinese moved elite and veteran divisions to Tibet from Chengalu and Lauzhou. On the 12th of October, Nehru ordered, "Clear Indian territory in the NEFA of Chinese invaders."

On the 14th of October, the Chinese issued a last warning. On the 20th of October, the Chinese attacked in the Chip-Chap Valley in Aksai-Chin and, in the east, captured both banks of the Namka Chu (river). There were skirmishes at Nathu La, and after four days of fierce fighting, the Chinese secured substantial portions of the disputed territory.

The Battle of the Namka Chu

On October 20, while the Indians waited near five bridges that spanned the Namka Chu, the Chinese crossed over from a point where the river was shallow and bypassed the defendants under the cover of darkness.

At 5.14 a.m., Chinese mortars opened up. The Chinese had cut the telephone lines. In those days, wirelesses were in short supply. At 6.30 a.m., they launched a surprise attack from the rear. The Indians were forced to abandon their position and flee. Some of them escaped into Bhutan. At the time of the Thang La confrontation, the Chinese held all the disputed territories but kept advancing into NEFA.

On October 22, at 12.25 a.m., the People's Liberation Army (PLA) attacked Wallong, situated on the McMahon Line, by mortars. The Indians held on for four hours but had to withdraw against the sheer weight of numbers of the Chinese soldiers.

On October 23, the Chinese were caught in a pass. The Indians opened fire with mortars and machineguns. Two hundred Chinese were killed. Nine Indians died. The company was told to withdraw, but Sepoy Piara Singh refused to do so and fought till death.

On October 25, there were clashes at Walong. When the ammunition finished, Sepoy Kewal Singh charged and fought hand to hand until he was killed.

On the western front, already most of the disputed territory was under Chinese control. By October 22, most of the posts north of Chishul had been taken.

On October 20, the Chinese took the Chip-Chap Valley, the Galwan Valley and Pengang So (lake).

The Galwan post had been besieged since August, but there had been no reinforcement or relief. All defenders there were either killed or captured.

Indian Western Command withdrew isolated posts to the southeast. In Siachen, Daulat Beg Oldi was also evacuated. This post was reopened in 1987-88. As this post was south of what China had laid claim to. It was also left alone by them.

On October 24, China advanced 16 kilometres south of the control line. There was four days of fierce fighting followed by three weeks of lull. The Indians had retreated to Se La and Bombdi La, which was heavily fortified and difficult to assault.

Negotiations fell through. The Chinese acknowledged the McMahon Line in NEFA, but they wanted the Mac Donald Line in Aksai-Chin to be recognized.

On November 14, fighting resumed. The Indians attacked Walong while the Chinese resumed military activity in Aksai-Chin and NEFA.

On the 17th of November, the PLA cut off supplies to Se La and Bombdi La, isolating 10,000 Indian troops. They had again achieved a surprise by attacking over the mountains instead of by the expected road.

On the 18th of November, the PLA attacked near Chishul. At 5.45 in the morning, they attacked Gurung Hill. They cut off communications. By 9 a.m., they made a direct attack and the Indians had to retreat.

The Chinese simultaneously attacked Rezang La at 6.55 a.m. This position was held by a mere 123 men, under Major Shaitan Singh. The men there fought to the last man. Over 1,000 Chinese died and 109 of the Indian defenders were killed. Nine survivors were severely injured. The Chinese gave decent burial to all the dead defenders.

Just when the troops were coming to grips with mountain warfare and calling for more troops, the Chinese declared a unilateral ceasefire.

The Indians suffered heavy casualties, especially at Rezang La. The Indian troops wanted to fight to the bitter end, but ceasefire was declared.

The PLA had reached the outskirts of Tezpur, in Assam. Civilians had been evacuated and prisons thrown open.

On the 19th of November, China reached its line of claim and declared unilateral ceasefire. In November 1962, the U.S. Air Force flew in supplies, but by the time these supplies reached, the war was already over. The world opinion was that all China wanted to show was that it would not leave what it considered its own. America decided that if China ever attacked India again, it would use nuclear weapons against it. Although this was the most colossal military debacle for India, there were many heroes of this war.

Subedar Joginder Singh, PVC

Subedar Joginder Singh, the winner of the Param Vir Chakra (PVC), was stationed in Tawang sector of NEFA with his platoon in a defensive position on a ridge in the Tongpeng La area on the Bum La axis. He and his platoon fought off three attacks by the Chinese. When their bullets finished, they charged with fixed bayonets. Finally, Subedar Joginder Singh was overpowered and captured. He refused amputation of his frostbitten foot and died in captivity. He was awarded the PVC posthumously.

Major Shaitan Singh, PVC

Major Shaitan Singh, PVC, was the hero of the Battle of Rezang La, near Chishul. At this battle, 100 Ahirs, led by a Rajput, died for India. On the 18th of November, early in the morning, Singh spotted the Chinese. When in spite of artillery and mortar shelling, the Chinese frontal attack failed, they attacked from the rear. The Indians let them have it with whatever they had. About 120 of the Chinese charged Number 7 Platoon, which by now was surrounded. About a dozen Kumaonies came out to fight hand to hand. The platoon fought till the last man. Platoon 8 also fought till its ammunition lasted.

Major Shaitan Singh showed exemplary courage by going from platoon to platoon, encouraging his men and exposing himself to enemy fire. He was seriously wounded by machine-gun fire but continued to fight. While he was being evacuated, he realised that the men carrying him were in danger. He ordered them to leave him and go. Reluctantly, they left him behind a boulder and went. He was decorated with the PVC, posthumously.

Major Dhan Singh Thapa, PVC

Major Dhan Singh Thapa, PVC, of 1st Battalion of 8th Gurkha, was the hero of Sirijap 1, which lies north of the Pengang So, in Ladakh. Born in a Chetri family of Shimla to P. S. Thapa, he joined 8th Gurkha Rifles on the 28th of August 1949.

Chetri 1, north of the Pengang Lake, in Ladakh, was vital for the defence of Chishul. It was held by a platoon of C Company under Major Dhan Singh Thapa. On the 20th of October 1962, the Chinese attacked this position. At 6 a.m., the Chinese opened a barrage of artillery fire upon this post. At 8.30, the entire area was set ablaze. Communication with headquarters was lost because the only wireless set was destroyed by a stray shell. Major Dhan Singh Thapa repulsed two attacks, inflicting heavy casualties upon the enemy. In the third attack, the Chinese used tanks. Major Thapa and his men fought till their ammunition lasted. Then, they came out of their bunkers and fought hand to hand until they were overpowered, and captured. Major

Dhan Singh Thapa was decorated with the PVC. He retired as a lieutenant colonel.

Rifle Man Jaswant Singh Rawat, MVC; Rifle Man Gopal, VC; and Lance Naik Trilok, VC

Rifleman Jaswant Singh Rawat, Maha Vir Chakra (MVC), Rifleman Gopal and Lance Naik Trilok, both Vir Chakras (VCs), were serving with the 4th Battalion of Garhwal Rifles at Nuranang, in NEFA. On the 17th of November, there were repeated assaults by the Chinese on their position. Rifleman Jaswant, Lance Naik Trilok and Rifleman Gopal went after the medium machine gun (MMG) of the Chinese, which was creating havoc. Then, within 12 metres of the MMG nest, they threw in a grenade, charged into the bunker and, killing a number of Chinese, captured the MMG. Jaswant now took the MMG and started crawling back. He and Trilok were hit fatally by Chinese automatic fire. Gopal was also wounded but managed to drag the MMG to the Indian post. This turned the course of the battle. The Chinese retreated, leaving 300 dead behind. Jaswant was decorated posthumously with an MVC while Trilok was decorated with a VC, also posthumously. Gopal was also decorated with a VC.

There is a Baba Jaswant Singh Rawat memorial in Tawang. Whosoever goes there has to stop and pay abeyance here. Jaswant and his colleagues had held on to this post for 72 hours. There are rumours that Jaswant was wounded and shot himself. Another tale says he was captured by the Chinese, who hanged him and then sent back his head along with a bronze bust of him. The place where this bust is located is known as Jaswant Garh.

Brigadier Hoshiar Singh

Brigadier Hoshiar Singh, the hero of Sela in NEFA, thwarted four attempts by the Chinese to overrun the position and beat them back on the 17th of November 1962. There were heavy losses on both sides. He was ordered to withdraw. He did not want to do this as he had adequate supplies for 10 days. There is a lot of confusion about who gave him orders to withdraw. But for the army, orders are orders. It was while he was retreating that the brigade major, Dutta, also the logistic staff officer of the brigade headquarters, got separated from the brigade commander. The retreating brigade was ambushed and the brigade commander, Brigadier Hoshiar Singh was killed. Sela would have been the ideal place to stop the Chinese advance, but why this order for retreat was given and by whom is still a mystery.

This was one war for which in spite of advance warning we were too complacent and not prepared. I remember as a child we were in Patna. There was mass hysteria, and the Indian public rose to the occasion. Ladies donated all their jewellery, and people gave everything, from money to labour, for free. Suddenly, planes full of troops on their way to NEFA started landing day and night at Patna, which had suddenly become a major halt on the way to NEFA. One rich landlord of Patna, Mr. T.P. Singh, out for his morning walk, dropped in on the airport. In those days, security checks were non-existent. He was horrified to find that our troops were going to the front to fight in snow in their summer clothes; had no proper shoes, only canvas sneakers, upon their feet; had obsolete rifles of Second World War vintage slung across their backs by *niwar*, with only five bullets issued per person; and had had no food for the past two days. On the spot, that gentleman signed a check for rupees 10,000, which was a lot in those days, and ordered a lunger to be opened at the airport so that every soldier who went through would at least get a hot meal.

This war brought out the fact about how complacent we had become. More attention was being paid in the armed forces to spit and polish instead of actual combat drill. Industries that were supposed to make ammunition and guns had been diverted for civil purposes. Our guns were obsolete, of Second World War vintage. The soldiers were never allowed to practice with live ammunition as it was considered too costly; as a result, most of the guns got jammed when they were fired in actual war. Again, we were so absurdly sure of the McMahon Line that we forgot it was nebulous and only on paper. The Maginot Line, in France, which the Germans went around without any resistance in the

Second World War when the Germans blitzkrieged to France, was better fortified but still failed to curb the German invasion; similarly, the McMahon line failed to curb the Chinese invasion.

The good thing about this war was that we got such a jolt that, after this, our politicians never again took the army for granted or neglected it by underplaying its importance in the defence of India.

References

1. Indiandefence (2012). *Indian War Heroes*. Retrieved from http://www.indiandefence.com/forums/military-forum/15140-indian-war-heros.html
2. Wikipedia (n.d.). *Dhan Singh Thapa*. Retrieved from http://en.wikipedia.org/wiki/Dhan_Singh_Thapa
3. Wikipedia (n.d.). *Hoshiar Singh*. Retrieved from http://en.wikipedia.org/wiki/Hoshiar_Singh
4. Wikipedia (n.d.). *Shaitan Singh*. Retrieved from http://en.wikipedia.org/wiki/Shaitan_Singh
5. Wikipedia (n.d.). *Sino-Indian War*. Retrieved from http://en.wikipedia.org/wiki/Sino-Indian_War

22 CHAPTER The 1965 Indo-Pak War

After the Chinese debacle in 1962, Pakistan wanted to take advantage of the low morale of India and its armed forces. On August 5, 1965, some 26,000 to 33,000 Pakistani troops dressed as locals crossed into Kashmir. By the end of August, the Pakistanis had captured Tithwal, Uri and Poonch. In retaliation, the Indians captured the Haji Pir Pass at a great loss of life. Unfortunately, later on, this was returned to the Pakistanis in the Treaty of Tashkent.

On September 1, 1965, Pakistan launched Operation Grand Slam to capture Akhnoor, in Jammu district. India used its air force to blunt and stop the Pakistani attack. The next day, Pakistan retaliated by attacking Indian bases in Kashmir and Punjab.

The Indians crossed the international border on September 6. 15th Infantry Division, under Major General Prasad, repulsed massive attacks at Ichogil Canal. At one point, the general was ambushed and had to leave his jeep and run. But then, he regathered his troops, recrossed Ichogil Canal, at Burki, and advanced till they were literally on the doorsteps of Lahore.

That was the time in between the rule of Nehru and Indira Gandhi. The diminutive Shastri ji was at the helm of the country. He was thin and short and looked so unassuming that all Indians wondered and despaired at what this tiny man would do in this crisis. Whenever he came on cinema screens in the mandatory news reels (there were no TVs then), people either laughed or shook their heads. But the tiny simpleton was made of tougher steel than anyone could have guessed. Not only did he not buckle down under pressure but he lifted up his diminutive arm and roared as loudly as a lion and declared that if the Pakistanis thought they would have breakfast in Pathankot and lunch in Delhi, they were mistaken. It would be us having breakfast in Lahore. After this declaration, every time his image flashed on the screen in the cinema halls, I remember every one breaking into cheers and clapping madly. It was something to behold.

The 1965 battle was another ding-dong battle. The Pakistanis took Khem Karan and Dograi. The Indians captured Batapore (of Bata shoe fame), lost it and recaptured it with heavy casualties.

On September 9, the Indians attacked Sialkot. Pakistan's 6th Armoured Division forced them back at Chawinda. Pakistan launched Operation Wind Up, pushing the Indians further back. Pakistan attacked at Khem Karan. Its intent was to capture Amritsar, then capture the bridge over the river Beas and then advance to Jalandhar over it.

The battle at Khem Karan was one of the fiercest and came to be known as the Battle of Asal Uttar. The area became known as Patton Nagar because of the number of the American Patton tanks used by Pakistan destroyed and abandoned there. In this battle, 32 tanks were destroyed or damaged.

In this war, the Indian Army suffered 3,000 casualties. Pakistan suffered 3,800 fatalitics. Indians captured 710 miles (1,800 km) of territory, while the Pakistanis captured 210 miles (550 km) of territory. The Indians captured fertile land in Sialkot, Lahore and Kashmir sectors. The Pakistanis captured land in the desert opposite Sindh, in Chhamb and near Kashmir.

This was the first war where the Indian Air Force fighters played a major part. Indians used Hawker Hunters, Indian-made Folland Gnats, deHavilland Vampires and EE Canberra bombers and had a squadron of MIG 21s.

The Pakistanis had 102 F-86 Sabres, 12 Star fighters, and 24 B-57 Canberra bombers. Pakistan was outnumbered 5:1. But because the Indian Air Force was split to guard against an attack from China, the two air forces were well matched. Neither side achieved air superiority. There was a stalemate.

This war saw some of the biggest tank battles. The Indian Centurian tank proved better than the more complex American-made Patton tank used by the Pakistanis.

This was the first war in which the navies of both countries also came into play.

On September 7, under operation Dwarka, a flotilla of Pakistan Navy, under Commander S.M. Anwar, bombed the Indian Navy's radar station at Dwarka, which lay 200 miles (300 km) south of Karachi.

Pakistan also claims that its submarine PNS *Ghazi* besieged INS *Vikrant*, the only aircraft carrier we had then, while it lay in Bombay (present-day Mumbai) Port. But actually, *Vikrant* was getting refitted at the port and was never threatened.

Pakistan also parachuted 135 Special Service Group (SSG) commandos on three airfields: Halwara, Pathankot and Adampur. Of them, 93 were taken prisoner and only 22 managed to return to Pakistan. Twenty of them were killed in encounters with the army, police and civilians. These included one of their commanders Major Khalid Butt. The commandos had no maps and no proper briefing, planning or preparation before being dropped. Most historians agree that in this war, India had the upper hand.

This war threw up many names. For the first time, two brothers, flying similar aircraft, were awarded the same medals for the same war. The Keelor brothers became household names.

Squadron Leader Denzil Keelor, VC, VSM, KC, AVSM

Denzil Keelor, born on the 27th of December 1933, was a part of No. 4 Squadron, which he later commanded. He was later awarded the Vishist Seva Medal (VSM), the Kirti Chakra and the Ativishist Seva Medal (AVSM). He joined the Indian Air Force on the 6th of November 1954 and rose to the rank of Air Marshal. After retirement, he worked as president of the YMCA for 10 years. Then, he became chairman of Special Olympics Bharat.

Denzil Keelor's first award was the Vir Chakra (VC), in 1965. The citation reads as follows:

> On 19th September 1965, Sqn Ldr Denzil Keelor was providing fighter escort to Mystere aircraft during a strike mission in the operations against Pakistan. His section of four Gnat aircraft was engaged by four enemy Sabre jet aircraft and the battle was fought at a height of less than 2,000 feet from the ground where enemy anti-aircraft guns were also active. Under his guidance, his subsection leader shot down a Sabre jet aircraft. Thereafter Sqn Ldr Keelor himself engaged another Sabre jet and crippled it. Throughout the operations, Sqn Ldr Keelor was a source of inspiration to his pilots and ground personnel. His courage and devotion to duty were in the best traditions of the Air Force. For this he was awarded the Vir Chakra. The Sabre kill by Denzil earned the Keelor family a unique distinction. Both the brothers now had Sabres to their credit and both earned the Veer Chakra, making it the first time brothers had won the Vir Chakra for identical feats.

In 1978, Keelor was awarded the Kirti Chakra. The citation reads as follows:

> Gp. Capt. Keelor who had rich and wide combat experience and the destruction of a Sabre aircraft to his credit, was flying a MiG-21 U trainer on 27 Mar 78, when due to structural failure the canopy of the aircraft detached and flew off. Gp Capt Keelor felt sudden decompression and loss of control, but managed to fly back to base and execute a safe emergency landing without the canopy. Later on 17 May 78, during firing trials one of the 23 mm Cannon Shells exploded causing extensive damage and total electrical failure to his aircraft. He successfully executed another safe landing back at his airbase.

Denzil had a younger brother, Trevor. Trevor was born on the 8th December 1934. Like his elder brother, Trevor also got decorated for the same war.

Flight Lieutenant Trevor Keelor, VSM, VC

Keelor was awarded the Vayu Sena Medal (VSM) in 1964. The citation reads as follows:

> On the 5th February 1964, Flt Lt Keelor was detailed to ferry a Gnat from Poona to Palam in a formation of five aircraft. The last part of the flight had to be undertaken at a height of 41,000 feet. While descending to land at Palam, he discovered, at a height of 15,000 feet that there was no response from the engine to the throttle movements. After informing the leader, Flt Lt Keelor immediately broke off the formation and attempted a landing at Palam, knowing fully well that previous attempts to force land a Gnat had resulted in fatal or serious injury to the pilot. With great presence of mind and careful handling, he accomplished the forced landing successfully without any damage to the aircraft. Flt Lt Trevor Keelor displayed courage, presence of mind and a high standard of professional skill in the best traditions of the Indian Air Force.

The following year, in 1965, Trevor Keelor was awarded the VC. The citation reads as follows:

> On 3rd September 1965, on receipt of a report that a formation of Pakistani fighters were circling over our Army position in the Chhamb Sector of J&K, a formation of Gnat aircraft was ordered to intercept the intruders. Approaching the area, Sq Ldr Trevor Keelor, who was a section leader in the Gnat formation, sighted enemy F-86 Sabre jets and engaged them in air battle. When the combat was in progress, F-104 Star fighters of the Pakistani Air Force also joined in. Unmindful of the numerical superiority of the enemy, Sq Ldr Keelor chased a Sabre jet and pressed home his attack until the enemy aircraft caught fire and disintegrated in the air. This was the first victory of our Air Force in the air battles against the Pakistani Air Force. In this operation, Sqn Ldr Keelor displayed courage and leadership of a high order in the best traditions of the Air Force.

Denzil Keelor was awarded the AVSM on January 26, 1986, and the Param Vishist Seva Medal (PVSM) on January 26, 1989.

Company Quarter Master Havildar Abdul Hameed, PVC

The most famous battle in the Khem Karan area was the Battle of Asal Uttar. In this battle, so many enemy tanks were destroyed and disabled that the area came to be known as Patton Nagar. Here, 97 Patton tanks were either destroyed or abandoned. Thirty-two Indian tanks were destroyed or damaged. It was at this battle that Havildar Abdul Hameed of Gazipur, in eastern UP, became a hero. Born on July 1, 1933, to a tailor's family at Dhampur village, in Gazipur district, he joined the Grenadiers on the 27th of December 1954. He took part in the 1962 War in North Eastern Frontier Area (NEFA) under Brigadier John Dalvi in the Battle of Namka Chu, where the Indians had been surrounded but many managed to break out and escape into Bhutan.

Abdul Hamid was the best 106 mm, recoilless rifle shot in the battalion. His battalion, 4 Grenadiers, along with three other battalions, formed a defence line between the village of Asal Uttar and Chima Village on the Khem Karan-Bhikiwind–Amritsar Road.

The battalion, after being forced back from Ichogil Canal, started digging in—hidden from view by cotton and sugarcane fields. On the 8th of September, the enemy made repeated attacks in the afternoon. Abdul Hamid destroyed two Patton tanks that day. Of all the silly things, the commander of one of them had stopped on the road and was asking him for directions.

On the 10th of September, at 0800 hours, a battalion of Pakistani armour supported by Pakistani tanks attacked the position of 4 Grenadiers. By 0900 hours, the enemy had penetrated the forward company's position. Abdul Hamid saw a group of Pakistanis heading towards his battalion defences. He moved out to a flank with his gun mounted on a jeep. Under intense enemy shelling and fire, he knocked out three Patton tanks. He was killed by the fourth one. Although officially he has been credited with the destruction of only three tanks, he did destroy another three on the 8th of September.

The citation for the Param Vir Chakra (PVC) awarded to him posthumously reads:

Company Quarter Master Havildar Abdul Hamid 4 Grenadiers (No 2639985)

At 0800 hours on 10 September 1965 Pakistan forces launched an attack with a regiment of Patton tanks on a vital area ahead of village Cheema on the Bhikiwind road in the Khem Karam Sector. Intense artillery shelling preceded the attack. The enemy tanks penetrated the forward position by 0900 hours. Realising the grave situation, Company Quarter Master Havildar Abdul Hamid who was commander of an RCL gun detachment moved out to a flanking position with his gun mounted on a Jeep, under intense enemy shelling and tank fire. Taking an advantageous position, he knocked out the leading enemy tank and then swiftly changing his position, he sent another tank up in flames. By this time the enemy tanks in the area spotted him and brought his jeep under concentrated machine-gun and high explosive fire. Undeterred, Company Quarter Master Havildar Abdul Hamid kept on firing on yet another enemy tank with his recoilless gun. While doing so, he was mortally wounded by an enemy high explosive shell.

Havildar Abdul Hamid's brave action inspired his comrades to put up a gallant fight and to beat back the heavy tank assault by the enemy. His complete disregard for his personal safety during the operation and his sustained acts of bravery in the face of constant enemy fire were a shining example not only to his unit but also to the whole division and were in the highest traditions of the Indian Army.

Lieutenant Colonel A.B. Tarapore, PVC

Lieutenant Colonel A.B. Tarapore, of the 17 Poona Horse, was awarded the PVC posthumously. Born on August 18, 1923, in Mumbai, he belonged to the illustrious family of one of the generals, General Ratanjiba, of Chatrapati Shivaji. Popularly known as Adi, he originally got commissioned in the infantry but was not happy. One day, when the battalion was being inspected by the commander-in-chief, Major General Edroos, a grenade fell into the bay area. Adi jumped in and threw it out. But it exploded, injuring him in the chest. The general congratulated him on his heroic act. Adi requested him to be transferred to the Armoured Corps. He then joined 1st Hyderabad Imperial Service Lancers. He also saw service in west Asia during the Second World War.

Lieutenant Colonel Ardeshir Burzarji Tarapore was awarded the highest war-time gallantry medal, the PVC, posthumously. The citation reads:

Lieutenant Colonel A.B. Tarapore,
Poona Horse (17 Horse) (IC-5565)

On 11 September 1965, the Poona Horse Regiment under the command of Lieutenant Colonel Ardeshir Burzarji Tarapore was assigned the task of delivering the main armoured thrust for capturing Phillora in the Sialkot Sector in Pakistan. As a preliminary to making a surprise attack on Philloira from the rear, the regiment was thrusting between Philloira and Chawinda when it was suddenly counter attacked by the enemy's heavy Armour from Wazirali. Lieutenant Colonel A.B. Tarapore, who was then at the head of his regiment, defied the enemy's charge, held his ground and gallantly attacked Philloira with one of his squadrons supported by an infantry battalion. Though under continuous enemy tank and artillery fire, Lieutenant Colonel A.B. Tarapore remained unperturbed throughout this action and when wounded refused to be evacuated.

On 14 September 1965, though still wounded he again led his regiment to capture Wazirali. Such was his grit and determination that unmindful of his injury, he again gallantly led his regiment and captured Jassoran and Butur-Dograndi on 16 September. His own tank was hit several times, but despite the odds he maintained his pivots in both these places and thereby allowed the supporting infantry to attack Chawinda from the rear.

Inspired by his leadership, the regiment fiercely attacked the enemy heavy armour destroying approximately 60 enemy tanks at a cost of only nine tank casualties, and when lieutenant Colonel A.B. Tarapore was mortally wounded the regiment continue to defy the enemy.

The valour displayed by lieutenant Colonel A.B. Tarapore in this heroic action, which lasted six days, was in keeping with the highest traditions of the Indian Army.

These were some of the names that became household names after the 1965 War, in which although neither side could claim outright victory, India definitely had the upper hand. Unfortunately, to the chagrin of the Indian Army, most of the hard won areas were returned to Pakistan after the Tashkent Treaty.

References

1. Wikipedia (n.d.). *Abdul Hamid (Soldier)*. Retrieved from http://en.wikipedia.org/wiki/Abdul_Hamid_(soldier)
2. Wikipedia (n.d.). *Ardeshir Tarapore*. Retrieved from http://en.wikipedia.org/wiki/Ardeshir_Tarapore
3. Wikipedia (n.d.). *Denzil Keelor*. Retrieved from http://en.wikipedia.org/wiki/Denzil_Keelor
4. Wikipedia (n.d.). *Indo-Pakistani War of 1965*. Retrieved from http://en.wikipedia.org/wiki/Indo-Pakistani_War_of_1965
5. Wikipedia (n.d.). *Trevor Keelor*. Retrieved from http://en.wikipedia.org/wiki/Trevor_Keelor

23
CHAPTER
1971, Bangladesh War

What Led Up to It

When, in 1970, the Awami League of East Pakistan won a simple victory in the first ever parliamentary election in Pakistan and won 167 seats out of 197, getting a majority in the lower house consisting of 313 seats, Sheikh Mujibur Rahman claimed the right to form the government. Zulfikar Ali Bhutto, the then prime minister of Pakistan, refused. He called in the army to suppress the protests and demonstrations that this decision had led to. General Yahya Khan was entrusted with the job of suppressing any dissent. The Pakistan Army cracked down on Dhaka on the night of March 25, 1971. Operation Searchlight was launched, whose aim was to destroy the intellectuals of East Pakistan.

On March 27, 1971, Zia ur Rahman, a major in the Pakistan Army, declared the independence of Bangladesh on behalf of Sheikh Mujibur Rahman, who had been put in prison in West Pakistan. The exiled Awami League formed a government in exile in Baidyanathala of Meherpur, East Pakistan Rifles, a paramilitary force, defected to the rebels.

Mukti Bahini (liberation army) was formed, consisting of Niyomito Bahini (regular forces) and Gono Bahini (guerrilla forces) under commander-in-chief General Mohammad Ataul Ghani Osmay.

West Pakistan made General Tikka Khan in-charge of the forces in East Pakistan. The brutal genocide that followed under him earned the general the name of the "Butcher of Bangladesh".

According to General Niazi, "The stark cruelty displayed by General Tikka Khan was more merciless than the massacres at Bukhara and Baghdad by Chengez Khan and Halaku Khan." Major General Farman commented, "The green land of East Pakistan was painted red", by Bengali blood.

Refugees started pouring into India. India appealed to the international community, but there was no response. On the 27th of March 1971, Prime Minister Indira Gandhi expressed full support for the freedom struggle of East Pakistan. Deciding that armed action would be required to end the genocide, India started recruitment and training in the various refugee camps for Mukti Bahini guerrillas.

India started a build up in the east, while in Pakistan, slogans like "Crush India!" and "Hang the traitor [Mujib]!" were being shouted. On the 23rd of November, Yahya Khan declared an emergency.

On December 3, a Sunday, at 5.40 p.m. approximately, Pakistan launched preemptive strikes against 11 Indian airfields in the north, including Adam Pur, Halwara, Amritsar and Agra. Here, the Taj Mahal had been camouflaged under burlap and twigs as it glowed like a beacon in the moonlight. Our airfields were ready for such a strike, and not much damage was done to them. The Indian air force retaliated the very same night, as soon as the craters on the runways were filled up and the runways were repaired.

Naval Operations

In this war, for the first time the Indian Navy played a major role also. In the western theatre, under Vice Admiral S.N. Kohli, the navy successfully attacked Karachi (Operation Trident). On the night of December 4-5, using missile boats, they sank the Pakistani destroyer PNS *Khyber* and minesweepers PNS *Muhafiz* and PNS *Shah Jahan* were badly damaged. The number of sailors killed and wounded amounted to 720.

Operation Trident was followed by Operation Python, on the night of December 7-8, in which missile boats again attacked Karachi and sank three Pakistani merchant ships and destroyed many fuel tanks on the shore, thus depriving the Pakistani forces of vital fuel.

In the eastern sector, Eastern Naval Command, under Vice Admiral Krishnan, blockaded and isolated East Pakistan, trapping the East Pakistan Navy and eight foreign merchant ships. From the 4th of December onwards, Sea Hawk fighters from INS *Vikrant* bombed the coastal ports of East Pakistan, including Chittagong and Cox's Bazar.

Pakistan sent PNS *Gazi*, which sank off the coast near Vishakhapatnam. Pakistani submarine PNS *Hangor* sank the Indian frigate INS *Khukri* in the Arabian Sea, in which 18 officers and 176 sailors died.

Pakistan lost 7 gunboats, 1 minesweeper, 1 submarine, 2 destroyers, 3 petro crafts of the Coast Guard, 18 cargo supply and communication vessels and Karachi docks were damaged badly. Three merchant navy ships—*Anwar Bakhsh*, *Pasni* and *Madhumali*—and ten smaller vessels were captured. According to Pakistani scholar Tariq Ali, the Pakistan Navy lost a third of its force in the war.

Air Operations

In the east, the small air contingent of three aircraft of the Pakistan Air Force's No. 14 Squadron was destroyed.

Pakistan used B-57s and C-130s. Indians used Canberras and An-12s. Pakistan used F-6s mainly in defence. It was helped by Jordon and Saudi Arabia, which gave it F-104s, and by Libya, which gave it F-86s.

Before hostilities ended on December 16, at 14.30 hours GMT, Indian planes had flown 1,978 sorties over East Pakistan and approximately 4,000 sorties over West Pakistan. Pakistan had flown 30 sorties in the east and 2,840 sorties in the west. India lost 65 aircraft but admits to only 54, out of which 27 were probably lost in aerial combat. Pakistan lost 72 aircraft but admits to only 51, in which 20 were lost to combat and 25 were lost to other reasons.

Army Operations

In the east, Indian forces joined up with the Mukti Bahini to form the Mitro Bahini (friendly forces). The tactics they used were to avoid confrontations and aim straight for Dhaka.

Lieutenant General Jagjit Singh Aurora led the thrust into East Pakistan, with 8th, 23rd and 57th Divisions. The Pakistan Air Force in the east was put out of commission within the first few days, and the Indian Navy had blockaded East Pakistan.

The Indians used the technique of blitzkrieg, i.e. exploiting the weakness of the enemy positions and bypassing opposition, like the Nazis (Guderion) had done in the Second World War. On the 16th of December, Pakistan formally surrendered. Before this, on the 14th of December, the Pakistan Army killed a large number of intellectuals, doctors, teachers and educated young men belonging to East Pakistan. They murdered the intelligentsia and threw them in mass graves. The instrument of surrender of Pakistani forces in East Pakistan was signed on the 16th of December 1971 at 16.31 Indian Standard Time at the Ramna Race Course in Dhaka by Lieutenant General Jagjit Singh Aurora and Lieutenant General A.A.K. Niazi. India took 90,000 prisoners of war, the highest number ever taken in a war.

The blitzkrieg had been hastened because there was fear of a Chinese attack. But both the United States and the USSR assured India that in case of a Chinese attack, they would take countermeasures. But the United States also encouraged Jordan, Iran and China to send help and military supplies to Pakistan. President Nixon asked Iran and Jordon to send F-86s, F-104s and F-5 fighter jets to the aid of Pakistan. The United States also sent USS *Enterprise*, an aircraft carrier, into the Bay of Bengal. It reached on the 11th of December but could not get into action. Although India was prepared, China refused to mobilise.

The 90,000 prisoners of war were released after the Shimla Agreement on July 2, 1972. General Yahya Khan resigned. Zulfikar Ali Bhutto, father of late Benazir Bhutto, took over. Pakistan had lost half of its navy, one-fourth of its air force and one-third of its army and nearly half of its territory. Bangladesh emerged as the fourth-most populous Muslim state in the world.

Sheikh Mujibur Rahman returned to Dhaka on the 10th of January 1972 and became the first president of Bangladesh and later became its prime minister.

Some of the names that became household names in this war were those of Lance Naik Albert Ekka, Param Vir Chakra (PVC); Flying Officer Nirmal Jit Sekhon, PVC; Colonel Hoshiar Singh, PVC; and Second Lieutenant Arun Khetrapal, PVC.

Albert Ekka, PVC

Albert Ekka was born on the 27th December 1942 at Jari village of Chandpur tehsil, in Ranchi district, now known as Gumla district of Bihar. Son of Julius Ekka, he was born in an Oraon Christian family. At the age of 20, he joined 14th Guard. His son Bhisent was just nine months old when Ekka died.

On the 3rd of December, 14th Guard was asked to capture a Pakistani position at Ganga Sagar near Akhaura, on the border of Tripura and Bangladesh. When men of the 14th Guard attacked the enemy position at 0400 hours on the 4th of December, they came under heavy shelling and small-arm firing. They still pushed on, and hand-to-hand fighting took place. Ekka saw a light machine gun (LMG) firing from a Pakistani bunker. Ekka charged the bunker, bayoneted two enemy soldiers and silenced the LMG. He got seriously wounded but continued advancing for another 1.5 kilometres, clearing bunkers and other obstacles. When they reached near their objective, a medium machine gun (MMG) opened up from the second story of a well-fortified building. Progress was halted, and there were heavy casualties.

Despite his injuries, Ekka crawled forward and on reaching near the building, threw in a hand grenade, killing one enemy soldier and injuring another. Still, the firing went on. Ekka scaled a sidewall, entered the bunker, bayoneted the enemy and silenced the MMG. He got badly injured and, later on, succumbed to his injuries, but only after they had captured their objective.

Ganga Sagar fell. The enemy were forced to vacate Akhaura. Albert Ekka was decorated with the PVC posthumously. The Bihar government issued a postage stamp commemorating his memory, and there is a major intersection named after him in

Ranchi, in front of Firayalal Store, named Albert Ekka Chowk, which also bears his statue. A block in Gumla also bears his name.

Flying Officer Nirmal Jit Singh Sekhon, PVC

Flying Officer Nirmal Jit Singh Sekhon, a Jat Sikh, was born on the 17th of July 1943 in the village of Isewal Dakha, in Ludhiana district of Punjab. Son of Warrant Officer Honorary Flight Lieutenant Tarlochan Singh Sekhon, he was commissioned in the Indian Air Force on June 4, 1967, as a flying officer. On December 14, he was posted with the 18th Squadron, known as "The Flying Bullets", at Srinagar and was flying the Folland Gnat Fighter and was the only one on readiness duty. When Srinagar was attacked by 6 Pakistan Air Force's F-86 jets, Flying Officer Sekhon took off under heavy fire and engaged the Sabres. He managed to hit one Sabre and set another ablaze. After a lengthy treetop battle, the other four Sabres hit him, and he was killed. Unfortunately, his body was never found. The Pakistani pilot who shot him down, later on, in an article, was all praises for this brave fighter pilot. Flying Officer Nirmal Jit Singh Sekhon was later decorated with PVC posthumously. He was the only Air Force officer to be decorated with this in this war.

Major Hoshiar Singh, PVC

Colonel Hoshiar Singh, PVC, was born on May 5, 1937, at Sirsana village in Sonipat district, in Haryana. The son of Chaudhary Hira Singh, he was commissioned in the Grenadiers on the 30th of June 1963. He saw action in NEFA in 1965.

The citation for his PVC reads as follows:

Major Hoshiar Singh 3 Grenadiers (IC-14608)

On 15 December 1971 a battalion of the Grenadiers was given the task of establishing a bridgehead across the Basantar river in the Shakargarh Sector. Major Hoshiar Singh was commanding the left forward company and he was ordered to capture the enemy locality of Jarpal. This was a well-fortified position and was held in strength by the enemy. During the assault, his company came under intense shelling and effective crossfire from enemy medium machine guns. Undeterred, he led the charge and captured the objective after a fierce hand-to-hand fight. The enemy reacted and put in three counterattacks on 16 December 1971, two of them supported by armour, Major Hoshiar Singh unmindful of the heavy shelling and tank fire went from trench to trench, motivating his command and encouraging his men to stand fast and fight. Inspired by his courage and dauntless leadership, his company repulsed all the attacks inflicting heavy casualties on the enemy. Again, on 17 December 1971 the enemy made another attack with a battalion supported by heavy artillery fire. Though seriously wounded by enemy shelling, Major Hoshiar Singh again went from trench to trench moving about in the open with utter disregard to his personal safety when an enemy shell landed near the medium machine gun post injuring the crew and rendering it inoperative. Major Hoshiar Singh, realizing the importance of machine-gun fire, immediately rushed to the machine-gun pit and though seriously wounded himself, manned the gun inflicting heavy casualties on the enemy. The attack was successfully repulsed and the enemy retreated leaving behind 85 dead including their Commanding Officer and three other officers. Though seriously wounded, Major Hoshiar Singh refused to be evacuated till the ceasefire. Throughout this operation, Major Hoshiar Singh displayed most conspicuous gallantry, indomitable fighting spirit and leadership in the highest traditions of the Army.

Major Hoshiar Singh retired as a colonel and died of natural causes in 1998.

Second Lieutenant Arun Khetarpal, PVC

Second Lieutenant Arun Khetarpal PVC was born on October 14, 1950, in Pune, in Maharashtra, and died on December 16, 1971. He was an excellent student, and his father, Brigadier M.L. Khetarpal, was also in the army. Arun Khetrapal was commissioned in June 1971 in 17 Poona Horse. This paltan, under 47 Infantry Brigade, saw action in the Sakargarh sector. Second Lieutenant Arun Khetarpal's citation reads:

Second Lieutenant Arun Khetarpal, PVC

On 16 December 1971, the squadron Commander of 'B' Squadron, the Poona Horse asked for reinforcements as the Pakistani armour that was superior in strength, counterattacked at Jarpal, in the Shakargarh Sector. On hearing this transmission, Second Lieutenant Khetarpal who was in 'A' Squadron, voluntarily moved along with his troop, to assist the other squadron. Enroute, while crossing the Basantar River, Second Lieutenant Arun Khetarpal and his troops came under fire from enemy strong points and RCL gun nests that were still holding out. Time was at a premium and as a critical situation was developing in the 'B' Squadron sector, Second Lieutenant Arun Khetarpal, threw caution to the winds and started attacking the impending enemy strong points by literally charging them, Overrunning the defence works with his tanks and capturing the enemy infantry and weapon crews at pistol point. In the course of one such daring attack one tank commander of his troop was killed. Second Lieutenant Arun Khetarpal continued to attack relentlessly until all enemy opposition was overcome and he broke through towards the 'B' Squadron position, just in time to see the enemy tanks pulling back after their initial probing attack on this squadron. He was so carried away by the wild enthusiasm of battle and the impetus of his own headlong dash that he started chasing the withdrawing tanks and even managed to shoot and destroy one. Soon thereafter, the enemy reformed with a squadron of armour for a second attack and this time they selected the sector held by Second Lieutenant Arun Khetarpal and two other tanks as the point for their main effort. A fierce tank fight ensued: ten enemy tanks were hit and destroyed of which Second Lieutenant Arun Khetarpal personally destroyed four, just then Second Lieutenant Arun Khetarpal was severely wounded. He was asked to abandon his tank but he realized that the enemy though badly decimated was continuing to advance in his sector of responsibility and if he abandoned his tank the enemy would break through, he gallantly fought on and destroyed another enemy tank. At this stage his tank received a second hit which resulted in the death of this gallant officer.

Second Lieutenant Arun Khetarpal was dead but he had, by his intrepid valour saved the day; the enemy was denied the breakthrough he was so desperately seeking. Not one enemy tank got through.

Second Lieutenant Arun Khetarpal had shown the best qualities of leadership, tenacity of purpose and the will to close in with the enemy. This was an act of courage and self-sacrifice far beyond the call of duty.

But this does not give the full picture. When ordered to abandon his burning tank by his senior officer, he radioed, "No, sir, I will not abandon my tank. My gun is still working and I will get these bastards." His tank got hit again, and he was fatally wounded. His valour saved the day. The enemy was denied the breakthrough. Not one enemy tank got through. Even the enemy praised him and paid him tribute.

Second Lieutenant Arun Khetarpal was decorated posthumously with PVC. At the Indian Military Academy, Dehradun, a building has been named after him. The main entrance there has also been named after him. At the National Defence Academy, Kharakwasla, Pune, the main grounds have been named after him. His tank, Augusta Jx 202, was restored and, at present, is on display at the Armoured Corps Centre and School at Ahmadnagar.

The last time this valiant young man had met his mother, just before his regiment left for the front, she had told him, "Fight like a lion, and don't come back a coward."

But the story of this young man and his family does not end here. In 2001, Brigadier Khetrapal, at the age of 81, went to visit his birthplace, Sargodha, in Pakistan. At Lahore airport, he was met by Brigadier Khwaja Mohammad Naser—who became his host and guide. Brigadier Khetrapal stayed with the family of Brigadier Naser for three days, and they were very kind and attentive to him. After three days, Brigadier Naser told him.

"Sir, I regret to tell you that your son died at my hands. Arun's courage was exemplary and he moved his tank with fearless courage and daring, totally unconcerned about his safety. Tank casualties were very high till finally there were just the two of us left facing one another. We both fired simultaneously. It was destined that I was to live and he had to die.

It was only later that I got to know how young he was and who he was. I had all along thought that I would ask your forgiveness, but in telling the story I realise there is nothing to forgive. Instead I salute your son for what he did at such a young age and I salute you too, because I know how he grew into such a young man. In the end it is character and values that matter."

Later on, he sent some photos of this trip of Brigadier Khetrapal to him with the following written behind the photos:

> "To: Brigadier M.L. Khetrapal, father of Shaheed Second Lieutenant Arun Khetrapal, PVC, who stood like an insurmountable rock, between the victory and failure, of the counterattack by the 'SPEARHEADS' 13th Lancers on 16th December 1971 in the battle of "Bara Pind" as we call it and battle of 'Basantar' as 17 Poona Horse remembers it—Khwaja Mohammad Naser, 13 Lancers, 2nd March 2001, Lahore, Pakistan."

Someone had rightly said, "Wars are created by politicians, Compounded by bureaucrats and fought by soldiers." Who loses? The common man and the families.

References

1. Wikipedia (n.d.). *Albert Ekka*. Retrieved from http://en.wikipedia.org/wiki/Albert_Ekka
2. Wikipedia (n.d.). *Arun Khetarpal*. Retrieved from http://en.wikipedia.org/wiki/Arun_Khetarpal
3. Wikipedia (n.d.). *Hoshiar Singh*. Retrieved from http://en.wikipedia.org/wiki/Hoshiar_Singh
4. Wikipedia (n.d.). *Indo-Pakistani War of 1971*. Retrieved from http://en.wikipedia.org/wiki/Indo-Pakistani_War_of_1971
5. Wikipedia (n.d.). *Nirmal Jit Singh Sekhon*. Retrieved from http://en.wikipedia.org/wiki/Nirmal_Jit_Singh_Sekhon

24

CHAPTER

The Kargil War

This was the fourth war fought between India and Pakistan. It was fought in the limited sector of Kargil in Kashmir and elsewhere along the Line of Control (LoC) from May through July of 1999. Like in 1948, Pakistani soldiers in the garb of Kashmiri militants and with some Kashmiri militants infiltrated across the LoC. India then launched Operation Vijay to clear the area.

This war was a prime example of high-altitude warfare in a mountainous terrain. It is the only example of direct conventional warfare between two nuclear powers. At first, Pakistan claimed that it was independent Kashmiri insurgents who were involved. But later, when casualties were examined and recorded statements by the Pakistani prime minister and the Pakistani chief of staff were revealed, they showed the involvement of Pakistani paramilitary forces led by General Ashraf Rashid.

Infiltration and fighting took place on a 160-kilometre-long stretch of ridge that overlooked the only road connecting Srinagar to Leh. Most posts in this area are 5,000 metres, or 16,000 feet, and more above the sea line, and some posts are even situated as high as 5,485 metres, or 18,000 feet, above sea level.

The enemy chose this area deliberately after much thinking as this area is mostly unoccupied during the harsh winter. Again, if you are occupying the peaks, the terrain acts like a natural fortification.

Kargil is just 173 kilometres from Pakistan's Skardu, which provided logistic support to Pakistani infiltrators. After their defeat in 1971, Pakistan was smarting with the humiliation of the defeat. During the 1980s, both sides suddenly realised that the Siachen Glacier was unoccupied. Both rushed their troops there, and conflict escalated in the area. In 1984, under Operation Meghdoot, India managed to seize most of the glacier. During the 1990s, there was tension and an escalation in terrorism in Kashmir.

The Siachen Glacier is one of the highest and ecologically worst battlefields in the world. There was an unwritten understanding between the two nations that during summers, they would occupy what they had occupied first, but during winters both sides would return to their bases as the terrain and climate were too harsh. But in 1998-99, Pakistan decided to ignore this. Under the code name Operation Badi, they sent paramilitary forces in the guise of mujahideen's to cut off Srinagar from Leh. The then chief of Pakistan Army, General Pervez Musharaf, who later went on to became the president, planned this operation.

In February 1999, Pakistan reoccupied not only its own winter posts but also some of the vacant Indian ones. Troops from Special Services Group, along with four to seven battalions of the Northern Light Infantry, were involved. Intrusions took place in the heights of the lower Mushkoh Valley; along the Marpo La ridge line; in Drass; in Kaksar, near Kargil; in Batalik sector, east of the Indus River; on heights above Chorbatala sector and the Turtok sector, south of Siachen area.

In the second week of May, a patrol led by Captain Saurabh Kalia was ambushed. The mutilated body of the young captain was sent back after a week. The government launched Operation Vijay. Because of the harsh terrain, the fight was not at the divisional level or the corp level but at battalion and regimental levels. The Indian Air Force (IAF) was also deployed. They launched Operation Safed-Sagar in support of the ground troops. But they were severely hampered not only by the high altitude and bad weather conditions but also by the orders of the government, which did not give them permission to cross the LoC to bomb enemy targets accurately.

The Indian Navy prepared itself to blockade Karachi harbour to stop supplies to Pakistan. The then prime minister of Pakistan, Nawaz Sharif, admitted that Pakistan was left with fuel only for six days more. National Highway 1D, which is the main supply route from Srinagar to Leh, came under heavy firing. India realised that it had to control the hills overlooking this vital road.

Pakistan used unmanned aerial vehicles (UAVs) for reconnaissance and also used U.S.-supplied AN/TPQ-36, which used fire-finder radars. The IAF used French-made Mirage 2000H to drop laser-guided bombs upon well-entrenched Pakistani positions. The IAF lost one MIG 27 to engine failure, and one MIG 21 fighter was shot down. One Mi-8 helicopter was lost to stinger missiles (SAMS).

Most attacks were made at night, when the wind-chill factor brought down the temperature to anywhere from –11 degrees to –15 degrees Celsius. Indian troops could have blockaded the supply routes of the Pakistani troops by crossing the LoC but both the IAF and the army were under strict orders not to do so lest the war escalated.

Within two months, 75%-80% of the occupied area and nearly all of the higher grounds were back with India. Pakistan appealed to the United States, but President Clinton refused to intervene until Pakistan withdrew from the Indian side of the LoC.

In the last week of July, on the 26th of July, as soon as Drass sector was cleared of intruders, fighting ceased.

In this war, the much-maligned Bofors guns proved their worth. Again, this was the first war where the media had a field day. The war was brought right into the drawing room of every house as the war correspondents of all major channels flew with our air force, joined our men in their bunkers and stayed and took part as much as they were allowed to in various operations. For the first time, right from day one, everything was covered by the papers and television channels. Here is a tabular form of what was reported.

May 3: Local shepherds report the first Pakistani intrusion into Kargil sector.

May 5: An Indian army patrol is sent to investigate; five soldiers, including Captain Saurabh Kalia, are captured and tortured to death.

May 9: Heavy shelling is done by Pakistan Army, damaging the ammunition dump at Kargil.

May 10: Infiltration is noticed in Drass, Kaksar and Mushkoh sectors.

Mid-May: Troops from Kashmir Valley are moved to Kargil sector by the Indian Army.

May 26: IAF launches air strike against infiltrators.

May 27: IAF loses one MIG 27 and one MIG 21; Flight Lieutenant Nachiketa is taken prisoner of war by Pakistan.

May 28: An M-17 helicopter of the IAF is shot down by Pakistan; four aircrew are dead.

June 1: Pakistan bombs National Highway 1A.

June 5: The Indian Army releases captured documents from three Pakistani soldiers showing Pakistan's involvement.

June 6: The Indian Army launches a major offensive in Kargil.

June 9: Two key points in Batalik sector are captured.

June 11: Intercepts of conversation between Pakistan Army chief, General Musharaf, and Lieutenant General Aziz Khan are released.

June 13: Tololing, in Drass sector, is secured.

June 15: Bill Clinton asks Nawaz Sharif on telephone to pull out.

June 29: The Indian Army captures two vital posts, Point 5060 and Point 5100, near Tiger Hill.

July 2: The Indian Army launches a three-pronged attack in Kargil.

July 4: Tiger Hill is recaptured after a fierce battle of 11 hours.

July 5: Drass is brought under control. Nawaz Sharif announces withdrawal from Kargil after meeting Bill Clinton.

July 7: Jabar Heights in Baltik sector is recaptured.

July 11: Pakistan begins pull out from Kargil. India captures key peaks in Batalik sector.

July 14: Indian prime minister, Atal Behari Vajpayee, declares Operation Vijay a success.

July 26: The conflict ends officially.

There were many gallantry award winners in this war who became household names. Some of their stories are given below.

Grenadier Yoginder Singh Yadav, PVC

Grenadier Yogender Singh Yadav, Param Vir Chakra (PVC), of 18 Grenadiers was a member of a ghatak platoon, which attacked Tiger Hill on July 4. The enemy had entrenched himself in bunkers right on top. The climb was almost vertical and covered in snow on top of a 16,500-foot-high cliff face. Grenadier Yadav led the assault. When the assault party was halfway up, the enemy opened fire. The platoon commander was killed, along with two others. In spite of being hit by three bullets, Yadav continued for a further 60 feet, until he reached the top. He crawled to the first bunker and lobbed a grenade in, killing four Pakistani soldiers and neutralising enemy fire. Yadav then charged the second bunker, along with two others, and in hand-to-hand combat, killed four more Pakistani soldiers. The platoon captured Tiger Hill. Originally, Yadav was given PVC posthumously, but later, it was found that he was alive and had been shifted to Srinagar Military Hospital.

Lieutenant M.K. Pandey, PVC

Lieutenant M.K. Pandey, PVC, was born on the 25th of June 1975 at Sitapur, in UP. The son of a small-time business man, Sri Gopi Chand Pandey, even during his SSB interview, when asked why he wanted to join the army, he had replied, "Because I want to win the Param Vir Chakra."

Lieutenant Pandey was involved in the attack on Jubar Top in the Khalubar Hills, in Batalik sector. On June 11, he forced back intruders in his sector. Then, he led his men to capture Jubar Top. He led his men along a narrow treacherous ridge. While they were still short of their objective, the enemy opened fire. Lieutenant Pandey surged ahead and charged through a hail of bullets, giving a full-throated battle cry. Wounded in the shoulder and leg, he still continued. He reached the first bunker, and there was ferocious hand-to-hand combat. He killed two enemy soldiers and cleared the bunker. Inspired by him, his troops also charged. Unmindful of his injuries, Pandey charged from bunker to bunker. At the last, and fourth, bunker, he lobbed in a grenade but got a burst on his forehead. His last words in Nepali were, "*Na chhodun* (Don't spare them)." Critically injured, he fell at the final bunker. He later succumbed to his injuries, but Khalubar and Jubar Top were captured. He was decorated with PVC posthumously.

Lieutenant Pandey was also a poet. In his personal diary, he had written, "If death strikes before I prove my blood, I promise (swear), I will kill death."

In the movie *LOC Kargil*, Ajay Devgan portrayed him.

Captain Vikram Batra, PVC

Captain Vikram Batra, PVC (posthumous), was born in a Punjabi Khatri family on September 9, 1974, at Ghuggar village near Palampur, in Himachal Pradesh. He was commissioned as a lieutenant in 13th J&K Rifles and was nicknamed "Sher Shah" for his unstinting courage.

Captain Batra had been set the task of capturing Point 5140. He decided to lead the assault from the back. They climbed a sheer cliff. But near the top, the enemy pinned them down with machine-gun fire. Batra, along with five men, continued climbing, reached the top and hurled two grenades and single-handedly killed three enemy soldiers in close combat. He was seriously injured but regrouped his men and continued his mission. Inspired by him, the soldiers of 13 J&K Rifles charged the enemy and recaptured Point 5140 at 3.30 a.m. on June 20.

Batra's company killed at least eight enemy soldiers and recovered a heavy machine gun.

After this, Point 5140, Point 5100, Point 4700, Junction Peak and Three Pimples were all captured. Along with his fellow captain Anuj Nayyar and his men, Batra captured Point 4750 and Point 4875. He was killed when he tried to rescue an injured Lieutenant Naveen and bring him back during an enemy encounter on Point 4875 in the early morning of July 7. Naveen pleaded with him to let him continue fighting. Batra said, "*Tu baal bacchedar hai! Hat ja peechey* (You are a family man and have a wife and children. Move back)." His last words were, "*Jai Mata Di*! (Salute to the mother goddess)."

Batra was made more famous by the interview he had given to Barkha Dutt of NDTV just a week before his death, in which he had said, "*Ya tou Tiranga lehra ke aunga, ya fir Tirangey main lipata hua awanga, lekin awanga zaroor* (Either I will fly the tricolour and return or I'll return wrapped in it, but return I will)."

Batra had a sense of humour also. His excited transmissions when they recaptured Point 5140 became famous as he shouted into the radio, "Sir, *yeh dil mangey more*! (Sir, this heart clamours for more)"—a reference to a cola commercial of those times.

He also once had a cheeky radio exchange with an enemy commander who challenged him. The Pakistani commander said, "Why have you come here, Sher Shah? You will not go back."

Batra replied, "We shall see within an hour who remains on top."

Another time, the enemy taunted him with, "Give us Madhuri Dixit and we will go back."

Said Batra, "Sorry, Madhuri is busy. From Madhuri, with love."

He was decorated with PVC posthumously. In the picture *LOC Kargil*, Abhishek Bachchan played the role of Captain Batra.

Captain Anuj Nayyar, MVC

Captain Anuj Nayyar was born on August 28, 1975, in Delhi. He was commissioned on June 1997 from Indian Military Academy in 17 Jat. He did his studies from Army Public School, Dhaula Kuan.

Nayyar's company was asked to capture Point 4875 at 15,990 feet above sea level, situated atop a mountain with very steep slopes. It was considered impractical to attack without aerial support. On July 6, in a last-ditch attempt Nayyar's company decided to go ahead without any aerial support. During the initial phase of the assault, the company commander was injured. The assault company split into two, one led by Captain Vikram Batra and the other by Captain Anuj Nayyar. On Point 4875, the Pakistanis had constructed several bunkers. Nayyar, with seven men, located four of them. While still ascending, Nayyar and his men came under heavy artillery and mortar firing. Nayyar's team counterattacked. In hand-to-hand combat, they forced Pakistani soldiers to retreat.

While they were attacking the last bunker, an enemy-rocket-propelled grenade fell upon Nayyar. Despite being injured, Nayyar continued to lead the men and succumbed to his injuries only after he had cleared the last bunker on Point 4875. All the men in his team also died. Two days later, Pakistan counterattacked. 'C' Company, under Captain Batra, successfully defended the position. During the entire battle, 46 regular members of the Pakistan Army and an unknown number of paramilitary troopers and militants died. India lost 11 men, including both Captain Batra and Captain Nayyar. This paved the way for the capture of Tiger Hill. Nayyar was awarded the Maha Vir Chakra (MVC) posthumously. In *LOC Kargil*, Saif Ali Khan played Anuj.

But there is no end to human greed. The father of this brave martyr, S.K. Nayyar, had to run from pillar to post to get the petrol station allotted to him for his brave son's deeds. People wanted bribe to do what should have been done on a priority. What a shame!

Major Mariappan Saravanan, VC

Major Mariappan Saravanan, Vir Chakra (VC), posthumous, the hero of Batalik, was born on the 10th of August 1972. He was commissioned into Bihar Regiment on the 11th of March 1995 from the Officers Training Academy (OTA), Chennai. His father was Lieutenant Colonel Adi Mariappan, who died in a road accident in Bangalore in 1989, while serving in Operation Pawan (OP) (Sri Lanka).

When war was declared in 1999, 1st Bihar moved from Assam to Kargil. On May 28, Major Saravanan was given the task of capturing the well-fortified Pakistani position at 14,229 feet (4,337 metres) in the Batalik sector. He and his men, in spite of heavy artillery and automatic weapon fire, launched the attack at 04 hours. They charged into a volley of bullets. Major Saravanan fired a rocket launcher, killing two enemy soldiers. He himself was hit by shrapnel but he continued fighting. His commanding officer ordered him to retreat saying, "Changez Khan, fall back!" (Changez Khan was his code name.)

Major Saravanan replied, "Not today, Sir. We are very close to the objective." After this, he killed two more enemy soldiers but at 6.30 was hit by a bullet in the head. He was probably the first officer from the Indian side to fall in the Kargil war. All the men with him were killed.

Mrs. Amirthavalli Mariappa, mother of Major Saravanan, has this to say, "I am often referred to as the mother of the Hero of Batalik. I am proud that my son kept vigil over the frontiers even after his death. I am proud that my son was the first officer martyr from the Indian Army, and the last to come back home."

His body lay in snow until the only survivor from his company, Jawan Shatrughan, after crawling back for 10 days, as he himself was injured, brought back news about him and later succumbed to gangrene from his own injuries. The last word Major Saravanana had said to his mother before he left for Kargil were, "Mummy, I'll get you the Vir Chakra." A special cover and cancellation was issued by the postal department on July 20, 2008, to commemorate the memory of Major Saravanana.

Squadron Leader Ajay Ahuja, VC

Squadron Leader Ahuja, VC, posthumous, born on May 22, 1963, in Kota, Rajasthan, was tortured and killed by the Pakistani forces. He was commissioned on June 11, 1985, in the IAF. He had flown MIG 23 fighter bombers and MIG 21 variants, as well as having done instructional flying. He had experience of over 1,000 hours. He was posted at Killi Bhisiana air base, at Bhatinda, in Punjab, and had just become the flight commander of Squadron Number 17, known as the Golden Arrow Squadron. This was a special photo-reconnaissance squadron when the Kargil conflict started.

On May 27, as part of Operation Safed Sagar, while on a photo-reconnaissance mission, after an engine flameout, Flight Lieutenant Nachiketa ejected out of his MIG 27. Squadron Leader Ahuja, instead of abandoning him, stayed flying nearby over enemy territory to help rescue, knowing fully well the danger of surface-to-air missiles hitting his craft. His 21MF fighter-C-1539 was hit by a shoulder-fixed FIM-92 stinger missile. He radioed, "Hercule, something has hit my plane, probably a missile hit cannot be ruled out. I am ejecting over... (location)."

Later, postmortem showed that he had landed safely but had been shot in cold blood. On August 15, 1999, he was awarded the VC posthumously. A statue of his has been erected near the crossing of the Bhatinda-Muktsar Road.

Rifleman Sanjay Kumar, PVC

Rifleman Sanjay Kumar, PVC, was the leading scout of a team tasked to capture area Flat Top. On July 4, they scaled the cliff leading to this area, and when they were just 150 metres from the bunkers, they were pinned down by machine-gun fire from one of the bunkers. Sanjay Kumar crawled along the top of a ledge along the flank and charged the enemy bunker through a hail of bullets. He got three bullets but carried on, and in the ensuing hand-to-hand fighting, killed three enemy soldiers. Picking up an enemy machine gun, Sanjay Kumar crawled to the next bunker and killed a few of the enemy soldiers and forced the enemy who had been taken by surprise to flee. Inspired by him, the rest of the platoon charged, assaulted and captured Area Flat Top. In *LOC Kargil*, Sunil Shetty plays the role of Sanjay Kumar. Sanjay Kumar is one of the three surviving PVCs from Himachal Pradesh. A simple person, when he won the medal, he could not believe it.

Major Rajesh Singh Adhikari, MVC

Major Rajesh Singh Adhikari, Maha Vir Chakra, posthumous, was born on the 25th of December 1970 at Nainital. He was commissioned into the infantry in the 18th Grenadiers. He was the second Indian officer to die in the Battle of Tololing, during the Kargil conflict.

On the 30th of May, Major Adhikari was asked to secure a foothold by capturing the forward spur in Tololing. This was a strongly fortified position of the enemy. The terrain, 15,000 feet in height, was treacherous, mountainous and covered with snow. While going towards their objective, they were fired upon from two bunkers by universal machine guns. Major Adhikari immediately directed the rocket launcher detachment to engage the enemy and rushed in and killed two of the enemy in close combat.

Major Adhikari was injured, but he refused to be evacuated and kept directing the medium machine gun (MMG) subunit. He charged at the second bunker and killed one more enemy at Tololing. Adhikari had received a letter from his wife the day before, but he had stuffed it into his pocket, saying he would read it in peace. He never managed to do so. When he charged the second bunker, killed the enemy and secured this, thus securing Tololing, a bullet hit him in the head. He died 20 metres from his objective after conquering it. He was decorated with the MVC posthumously.

Captain Vijyant Thapar, VC

Captain Vijyant Thapar, VC, posthumous, was a fourth-generation officer, born at Nangal, in Punjab, on December 26, 1976. He belonged to Noida, in UP. Colonel V.N. Thapar, his father, was posted at Pathankot, in Punjab, in an armoured brigade when the boy was born, and he promptly named him Vijyant after the main battle tank of the army.

Vijyant was a bright student and, in IMA, won the silver medal in his first term and the gold medal for water polo. He was commissioned on December 12, 1998, in 2nd Rajputana Rifles. While serving in Kupwara, he faced two difficult and dangerous encounters. Here, he met a six-year-old girl, Ruksana, who had become withdrawn and mute after seeing her father being killed in front of her eyes. Vijyant sort of adopted her and even in his last letter to his parents asked them to keep looking after her and to keep sending her rupees 50 a month. The citation for him reads as follows:

Vir Chakra Citation

On 28 June 1999 Captain Vijyant Thapar was commanding the Leading platoon of Alfa Company, which was tasked to assault area Knoll in Drass Sector from the north during Operation Vijay. While advancing, the platoon was hit by accurate enemy artillery barrage and it suffered heavy casualties. Captain Thapar organized evacuation of the casualties and quickly rallied his shell-shocked platoon for the attack. Personally leading the attack from the Northern face against enemy's Medium Machine Gun fire, which was holding up the Company's assault, he fearlessly charged at the enemy position firing from the hip and throwing grenades. During this act, he was grievously injured in the hand and stomach but continued to advance ordering his men to follow him. Roused by the actions of their young Platoon Commander barely out of the Academy, the platoon charged up the hill against the dominating enemy position. This audacious action unnerved and forced the enemy to abandon a tactically superior position. The officer, however, succumbed to his injuries.

Captain Vijyant Thapar, thus, displayed remarkable cool, raw courage and exemplary valor and made the supreme sacrifice while facing the enemy.

The last letter Vijyant wrote to his parents is one of the most touching letters this author has ever read. A typical fauji style letter, it reads:

"Dearest Papa Mama Birdie (younger brother) and Grany,

By the time you get this letter I'll be observing you from the sky enjoying the hospitality of Apsaras.

I have no regrets. In fact, even if I become a human again I'll join the army and fight for my nation.

If you can, please come and see where the Indian army fought for your tomorrow.

As far as the unit is concerned the new chaps should be told about this sacrifice. I hope my photo will be kept in the 'A' coy mandir with Karni Mata.

Whatever organ can be taken should be done.

Contribute some money to orphanage and keep giving 50/- Rs. to Ruksana per month and meet Yogi Baba.

Best of luck to Birdie, never forget this sacrifice of these men. Papa you should feel proud. Mama so should you, meet... (I loved her). Mamaji forgive me for every thing wrong I did.

O.K. then its time for me to join my clan of the Dirty Dozen. My aslt (assault) party has 12 chaps.

Best of Luck to you all.

Live Life King Size, your's

Robin."

Vijyant Thapar was only 22 years old when he made the supreme sacrifice. When I saw the original letter in 1999, it brought tears to my eyes. Vijyant's funeral was attended by more than one lakh people in Noida. A road has been named after him in Noida.

References

1. Captainvijyantthapar (n.d.). *His Last Letter*. Retrieved from http://www.captainvijyantthapar.com/lastletter.html
2. Ikashmir (n.d.). *Shaheed Major Rajesh Singh Adhikari*. Retrieved from http://ikashmir.net/kargilheroes/adhikari.html
3. *India Today* (1999). *Coming Home*. Retrieved from www.india-today.com/itoday/28061999/rajesh.html
4. Wikipedia (n.d.). *Ajay Ahuja*. Retrieved from http://en.wikipedia.org/wiki/Ajay_Ahuja

5. Wikipedia (n.d.). *Anuj Nayyar*. Retrieved from http://en.wikipedia.org/wiki/Anuj_Nayyar
6. Wikipedia (n.d.). *Kargil War*. Retrieved from http://en.wikipedia.org/wiki/Kargil_War
7. Wikipedia (n.d.). *Manoj Kumar Pandey*. Retrieved from http://en.wikipedia.org/wiki/Manoj_Kumar_Pandey
8. Wikipedia (n.d.). *Mariappan Saravanan*. Retrieved from http://en.wikipedia.org/wiki/Mariappan_Saravanan
9. Wikipedia (n.d.). *Rajesh Singh Adhikari*. Retrieved from http://en.wikipedia.org/wiki/Rajesh_Singh_Adhikari
10. Wikipedia (n.d.). *Vijyant Thapar*. Retrieved from http://en.wikipedia.org/wiki/Vijyant_Thapar
11. Wikipedia (n.d.). *Vikram Batra*. Retrieved from http://en.wikipedia.org/wiki/Vikram_Batra
12. Wikipedia (n.d.). *Yogendra Singh Yadav*. Retrieved from http://en.wikipedia.org/wiki/Yogendra_Singh_Yadav